Getting A Life

About the author:

Dana W. is actively involved with helping recovering young people and works as an activist on issues such as homelessness, the oppression of women and people of color, and environmental issues.

About the illustrator:

Larry England began his career in the visual arts as a commercial artist and designer. He now teaches television production to high school kids, many of whom end up as subjects for his cartoons. He continues to do free-lance illustrations and works with his wife, Sherry, a face painter, as a caricaturist at conventions and fairs. He's also a published author and father of two grown sons.

Getting A Life

The Young Person's Guide to Drug-Free Living

Dana W.

Illustrated By
Larry England

HAZELDEN®

First published October 1990.

ISBN: 0-89486-720-2

Library of Congress Catalog Card Number: 90-82494

Printed in the United States of America.

Editor's note:
    Hazelden Educational Materials offers a variety of
information on chemical dependency and related areas.
Our publications do not necessarily represent Hazelden
or its programs, nor do they officially speak for any
Twelve Step organization.
    The stories of people in this book are real. In all
cases, names have been changed, and in many cases, the
circumstances have been changed to protect anonymity.
    The Twelve Steps and Twelve Traditions are reprinted
and adapted with permission of Alcoholics Anonymous
World Services, Inc. Permission to reprint and adapt the
Twelve Steps and Twelve Traditions does not mean that
AA has reviewed or approved the content of this publica-
tion, nor that AA agrees with the views expressed herein.
AA is a program of recovery from alcoholism. Use of the
Twelve Steps and Twelve Traditions in connection with
programs and activities which are patterned after AA but
which address other problems does not imply otherwise.

Contents

Acknowledgments

I would like to thank Jim Heaslip, Jane Pavkovich, Steve Lantz, Bruce Stellmach, and Jerry Johnson. You are all so very wise. A very special thank you goes to all of the recovering people who allowed me into their lives. (You know who you are.) Others who deserve credit and a thank you are my husband, family, and friends, and of course, Sid Farrar, my editor. Thank you, thank you, thank you.

Introduction

So you've decided to go straight. Or maybe you haven't really decided yet; that's okay. It doesn't really matter where you're at as long as you're willing to keep an open mind.

First, let me tell you a little bit about myself. My name is Dana and I'm an alcoholic and drug addict. My father is also alcoholic and he and my mother were divorced when I was ten. I started using when I was eleven. I went through treatment when I was seventeen. At that time, the thought of going straight seemed ridiculous. My drug use was my whole identity. I thought if I didn't use, I wouldn't know who I was anymore. No thank you. Luckily, I got smart and decided to give the program a try. I'd be lying if I told you it was easy.

There were times when getting drug-free was total emotional torture. But I lived to talk about it, and now that I've put in some straight time, I can say that I'm grateful. Every good thing I have in my life today I have because I'm straight. And I do mean *every* one.

I wrote this book to give you an idea of what you're in for when you go straight — the good and the bad. I'll promise you two things: (1) I'll try not to preach, and (2) I'll let other recovering young people do most of the talking.

Before we begin, the first chapter, "Inside Treatment," is for those of you who are in a treatment program now or are thinking about going into one. If you've already finished treatment, you might want to read it for old time's sake, or you can skip to Chapter 2, "Life After Treatment."

So . . . let's get started.

Good Luck!

Inside Treatment, *Or* What's a Nice Person Like Me Doing in a Place Like This?

Am I Having a Bad Dream?

No, you're not. This is real. You are in treatment for chemical dependency. Go ahead, feel free to pinch yourself.

You probably never figured you'd find yourself in this situation and are wondering what happened. . . . Just what went wrong that you'd end up in a place like this?

Well, sit back, fasten your seat belt, and relax as we go over some of the highlights that your treatment experience will probably include.

I know you probably don't believe it now, but treatment can be one of the richest and most rewarding experiences you'll ever have. No kidding!

Since all programs are a little different, what's described in this chapter may not describe your treatment program exactly. You may be in an outpatient program where you live at home and come in just for groups. Or you may live in a dorm or a hospital and be involved in an intensive inpatient program. Programs can last anywhere from two to forty weeks and can include many different features, but there are some common elements that we'll try to touch on in this chapter.

How Did I End up in Treatment?

Obviously, you are in treatment because your alcohol or other drug use is causing problems in your life.

People get into treatment in a variety of ways.

You can get into treatment in any one of a variety of ways. You may have been court ordered to complete treatment because of a Driving While Intoxicated offense or some other run-in with the law. Perhaps you started having serious problems at school or at home and a teacher, guidance counselor, or your parents brought you in. Or you may have decided for yourself that you needed help. In some way or another, you're having serious problems in your life that, there's reason to believe, stem from your chemical use.

There's a popular myth that an alcoholic or addict has to "want" help to go straight. Of course, it's easier when you want help, but even if you enter treatment against your will, you can still successfully complete treatment and stop using.

2

Most of us don't even realize we have a problem until we're put in a setting where we're forced to look at our chemical use. This brings us to one of the first big barriers to getting help for just about anybody addicted to chemicals.

The "D" Word . . . That's Right, Denial

Denial. It's one of the most common symptoms of chemical dependency. It's really bizarre if you think about it. I mean, when people are diagnosed with almost any other disease, they usually don't, for very long, deny that it exists and continue the very behavior that brought on their problems. But an alcoholic or other drug addict will usually be the last to admit to having a problem.

Denial can be fatal. Chemical dependency is a progressive disease, which means it's only going to get worse if nothing is done about it. Most people with this disease either go straight, that is, abstain from using *any* drugs (including alcohol), go insane, or die from it.

As you become involved in your treatment program and are evaluating your past chemical use, it's time to start being completely honest with yourself.

Tammy:

(A sixteen-year-old with a hard-core biker image.)

"A friend and I stole a purse from a neighbor of mine. We took all the money out of it and still needed more money, so we tried to forge one of the checks in it and got busted.

"It's crazy, because we took the purse so we could get money *for drugs,* we were intending to *buy drugs* with money from the forged check, and we were *on drugs* when we stole it; but I never thought I had a problem with drugs."

Tim:

(An eighteen-year-old with one year's sobriety, who is thinking about a career in advertising.)

"My parents were into as much denial as I was. It was a real battle. I took tests while I was in treatment, with questions like, 'Have you ever had a time when you couldn't remember what happened when you were drinking?' My folks would say things like, 'You know, I think most people have had that happen to them. I think most people would answer yes to that question.'

"It was tough because I wanted to think that I didn't have a problem and that I was no different from anybody else with my drinking. I mean who *wants* to be an alcoholic? Who wants a disease?

"What was really weird, though, was that once I had taken the First Step, you know, of Alcoholics Anonymous and admitted to myself that I was an alcoholic, my parents started to break through their denial."

Marty:

(A sixteen-year-old who is just getting out of treatment.)

"Denial! Oh man, did I go through denial! We're talkin' major league. I suppose, in a way, I still go through it. The biggest problem I have is with head games. You know, I try to intellectualize everything. I tell myself things like, 'I can't be a drug addict. I have always been on time to work, haven't I? I've never totaled my car, have I?' It's just total B.S.! The mind is very powerful and it'll do whatever it takes to get you out of feeling any kind of pain, so be warned.

"I guess all I've got to say is that if you've gotten into enough trouble to end up in a place like this, there's probably something that's not quite right in your life and you better start taking a look at it."

Okay, I'm Here. So Now What?

During the first few days of treatment, you're going to go through an orientation period. This will also be a period of *detoxification*, while you rid your mind and body of the chemicals you've been using. Some of you may go through more intense detoxification than others, and the length of this period will depend on how fried you are from all the poisons you've been putting into your body. Just about all of us have messed up our brain chemistry to some degree and we'll need some time to get cleaned out.

When you're ready, you'll be told a little bit about what your treatment program will be like, and you'll be introduced to the staff and the other young people. You may start going to groups where you talk with other young people about your chemical use. And, for a while, you might get your vital signs (blood pressure, pulse, temperature) checked every four to six hours.

. . . they will usually check your vital signs.

More than likely, sometime during the first three days, you'll be thoroughly grilled by a staff member about your chemical use. How much did you use? How often? Where? Did you ever try to quit but couldn't? Were you using more to get the same high? What events finally led up to your coming into treatment? And, like everything that's going to come out in treatment, your answers will be strictly confidential.

Ashanti:

(A seventeen-year-old who goes to an inner-city high school and plans to go to college after graduation.)

"The second night I was in treatment the counselors started asking me about how much I used and that kind of thing. They were really specific. I mean, they wanted to know a week by week description, all the way back to when I very first started! I couldn't believe it. I was amazed that I could even remember.

"Well anyway, I was totally honest. I figured, *I got nothin' to hide. I don't get high any more than anyone else I know, so what the hell.*

"After I was done, I went back to my room and everything that we had talked about started to sink in. I started thinking about how much I drank each week, and about all the so-called recreational drugs that I took, and how often I got high — and it just kind of blew me away. I never really thought about it before. It definitely was not normal or social use. Once that hit me, there was no denying it. I mean, this *is* a problem."

It'll probably be sometime during this first few days that you'll learn about chemical dependency as a disease, and begin to find out about Alcoholics Anonymous or Narcotics Anonymous and the Twelve Steps for recovery that are the backbone of most treatment programs.

Chemical dependency, or drug addiction (which includes alcoholism), is an incurable illness, but it *is* treatable. The way we are able to lead a normal, even happy life again is through total abstinence and the support of AA, NA, or some other Twelve Step recovery group. In treatment, we have to learn early on that we stay straight One Day at a Time.

Let's Say I Live Through The First Few Days. Then What?

The Evaluation Period

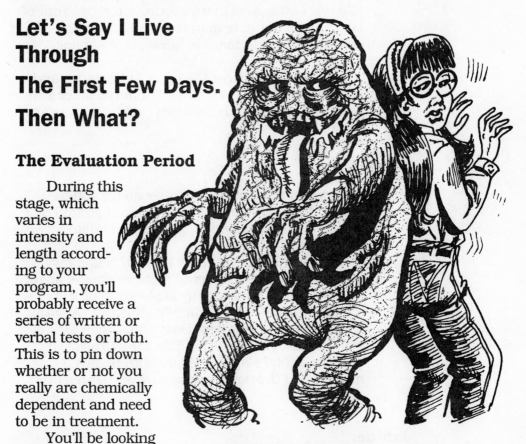

You'll be looking at your past . . .

During this stage, which varies in intensity and length according to your program, you'll probably receive a series of written or verbal tests or both. This is to pin down whether or not you really are chemically dependent and need to be in treatment.

You'll be looking at your past and your chemical use, and you'll have a chance to decide for yourself if your use has caused unmanageability in your life. In order to begin recovery, *you* have to believe that you are chemically dependent, not that you're just using drugs to get through a rough time and can quit once things lighten up.

Usually, you will have one or more meetings with your family to look at the behavior that brought you into treatment. You will also look at how your chemical use has caused problems in your family.

Teresa:

"I was going to lie my way through treatment. I told one of the guys in my group, 'I'm getting out of here. I'll be out of here in two weeks.' He just shook his head at me. He knew I'd be staying.

"Once I started to hear the other kids' stories and do my assignments, I could tell that the other kids were just like me. That's when I realized I was an addict."

Tyler:

"Looking at my past was hard — all the rotten things that I had done to people and that kind of thing. I just had so much shame and guilt.

"I think the thing that really broke through my denial was when I answered a questionnaire about all the different areas of my life — you know, social, spiritual, mental, family, physical. Anyway, one of the questions was 'How would each area of your life be different if you didn't use drugs?' It was like a total slap in the face with reality. I mean, I had the power to improve *every* area of my life!"

Janine:

"I was so pissed off at my folks for putting me in treatment. The whole first two weeks I was in, I couldn't even talk to them without it ending up in a big fight. It seemed like everything they were saying was just a bunch of lies, you know, like I was being plotted against. I couldn't deal with it. I didn't work on anything — any issues at all.

8

"Then, during my evaluation, I was just going through my usual B.S. and I turned to look at my mom and she just burst out crying. She was hurting so bad. Once I got in touch with the hurt she was feeling, it made all the difference in my recovery. I had pulled so much crap on them . . . stolen from them, lied to them. I really had a lot to deal with."

It'll probably be sometime during your evaluation period, if it's determined that you're chemically dependent, that you'll complete the First Step of the AA program. Step One is:

We admitted we were powerless over alcohol [or in NA, "over our addiction"] — that our lives had become unmanageable.

Taking the First Step means admitting that you are out of control when you use and that your use has caused problems in your life.

At the end of an evaluation period, you may have a meeting with the staff and your parents. At this meeting, the staff will tell you what they've learned from your tests, your behavior, and your interview, and you will tell them what you've learned about yourself. It is also at this meeting that a decision may be reached about whether you need to stay for the rest of the treatment program, go home, or go somewhere for a different kind of help.

To stay in treatment means you'll have to deal with some very painful issues in your life. That's why it's common to want to leave treatment at this stage — even after you've taken your First Step. But if you can hang in there, the best is yet to come. Now begins the real work and the chance for some real payoffs.

What Happens If I Decide To Complete the Treatment Program?

You probably will have already begun to attend groups and started to use some of the services (for example, individual counseling, medical consultation) that treatment offers during the evaluation period. If it's decided that you need to complete the treatment program, you'll continue with one or more therapy approaches.

Group Therapy — Also Known as Beyond Hell

Your first impression may be that the purpose of group is to see how much emotional torture the human mind and body can endure. Well, that's only partly true!

In group you meet from three to six times a week

with other young people and one or two counselors. In this setting, you'll work on issues in your life, such as family and peer relationships, school performance, and your attitudes and behaviors. You'll look closely at how these areas of your life broke down because of your chemical use, and how the bad feelings that came out of these problems created a vicious circle, feeding into your using more and more chemicals. You'll learn to start recognizing and dealing with feelings you've probably hidden or expressed in harmful or confused ways because of your addiction. Group members are usually encouraged to confront and challenge each other to cut through all the mind games that come with being an addict.

You may be given assignments and goals to accomplish both during and outside of the group. Group therapy is where you'll probably get some of your most important work done. You'll be with others who have been through some of the same things you have, which makes it easier to learn how to give and get the support you'll need to stay sober.

April:

"I just dreaded going to group! It was weird because, on the outside, I'd be smiling and joking all the time, but on the inside, I was petrified and going through total emotional torture.

"I was always raised to be a 'good little girl.' You know what I mean? I was always taking care of someone and always happy. I was like some kind of elf, cracking jokes and spreading sunshine all over! I wanted everyone to like me.

"Anyway, the best thing that I got out of group was that I learned to show my anger. If somebody does something that makes me mad, I let the person know. It's great. If I'm in a bad mood, it's okay to be that way; I don't have to medicate it. It's so important to get in touch with your feelings.

11

"Until I went through treatment, I was just numb. I don't really remember feeling anything. You need to get in touch with your feelings. Because if you don't learn to identify and express what you're feeling, you'll keep it pent up inside and it will eat at you. You'll be feelin' rotten, so you'll want to numb yourself out. If you express what you're feeling, you can put it behind you and forget it.

"When I first started showing my anger, I felt so guilty afterwards, like *Oh no, they're not going to like me anymore.* But then I just expressed that guilt too. It feels uncomfortable at first, but it's so worth it, and believe me, it gets easier."

Family Group

The members of your family will have their own problems to work on too. When one family member is an alcoholic or other drug addict, the other family members often take on a role in reaction to the addict's behavior. Chemical dependency affects the entire family, so it's important that your family be involved in the recovery process, if possible.

Many programs hold some group sessions that include family members. Family group will usually include you and your family, other young people and their families, and one or more counselors.

During these sessions, you'll have a chance to learn to communicate better with your family. This is accomplished in some settings with assignments that teach you and other family members how to share your true feelings with each other.

Some treatment centers offer a family day or family weekend during which the addict's concerned friends and relatives can learn about themselves in the same way as the addicted person is learning about his or her behavior.

Another reason for your family to be involved is so you'll have a supportive environment to go home to. This doesn't always happen, though, since some families are just not ready for help. It makes it harder if they aren't, but you can still recover if you practice honesty during treatment and learn to get support when you leave, from peers and from AA or NA.

Dennis:

(A seventeen-year-old who has a week of treatment left.)

"My family just totally blew off family groups. They hardly ever came, and when they did come, they didn't want to confront anything. They just didn't see that they needed to be a part of this. It's pretty unhealthy for me, that's why I'm going to a halfway house."

Janet:

"Family group was the best part of treatment. It just went great for me. My whole family came every week, even my brothers and sisters. We got a chance to get everything out in the open — all the things that we resented about each other — and all the things we liked and appreciated. We were able to start fresh and put the past behind us."

Mary:

"My stepdad has always been super negative. I had so much anger inside of me about it, and I never told him because I didn't want to make waves or upset my mom — until I went to treatment.

"In family group I got a chance to tell him how I really felt. I don't know if he's really changed all that much, but that doesn't really matter. All I know is that I am dealing with it a lot better.

"When I told him, in group, how angry and hurt I was, I felt like a huge weight had been lifted from my shoulders and it really helped my mom out too. Like I said, I don't think it really changed my stepdad much, but now my mom and I can talk to each other like friends. She gets fed up with him sometimes too.

"All I got to say to anybody who is going through family group now is, take advantage of the time you have there, because you're really laying the groundwork for your time at home."

Christopher:

"If it wasn't for family group, I don't think that my brother, Cal, would have ever realized that he had a problem with booze. After going through everything with me in group, he decided to go through treatment himself. We've never been closer."

Melody:

"We used to kid around that the best thing about family group is that you get to see your family go through as much torture as you had been through all week. Really, though, it helped my folks a lot.

"When I was using, my parents were *such* enablers! They *wanted* to trust me and they *wanted* to take care of me. It was bad.

"They learned a lot during family group and the family weekend. It was hard for them, but when I got home, they held me responsible for my actions.

"It was probably harder on me than it was on them, because I had gotten pretty used to getting

my own way and pressing their buttons, but I'm
far better for my new behavior. Definitely."

Other Stuff

Individual Therapy

In most settings, some individual therapy is available
where you meet with a counselor by yourself. This gives
you an opportunity to discuss any problems you may be
having that are too hard to talk about in group. The
counselor can give you feedback as to how you're
progressing and help you define and evaluate your
treatment plan.

School

If your treatment stay is during the school year and
you're in inpatient treatment, you may attend school at
the treatment center. Often, schoolwork is scheduled
from two to four hours a day to keep you from falling
behind. Some treatment centers allow you a pass to go to
your regular school classes or to visit your teachers.

Occupational Therapy

Some programs make occupational therapy available
once or twice a week. During this time, you'll have a
chance to learn the skills necessary to get and keep a job.
This may include some testing or counseling to help you
explore your career interests.

Pastoral Services

There may be clergy available to assist with spiritual
questions or problems. Religious services usually are
available upon request.

The B.S. Table

In between groups and classes, there's usually a lounge area where everyone can sit around and B.S. Sometimes this may be the easiest time for you to discuss an issue until you can take it to group, but it's important that this not become a substitute for group.

Recreational Therapy

Recreational therapy can include everything from team sports, playing cards, group exercise, swimming, bowling, socializing, or just working out on a punching

bag. Besides being a break from the stress of treatment, this is a chance to have some fun and be with other people while sober. For many of us, this is something we've either forgotten or may have never even learned.

Passes

Some inpatient treatment centers will give weekend passes or something similar. With a pass, you can go home for a weekend and test your new sobriety. It will give you an opportunity to see how you handle different situations without using.

Bob:

(A twenty-year-old who left treatment on his first weekend pass.)

"My first day out, I went to the mall, you know, just to do some shopping and check things out.

"I ran into two of my using friends and they were on their way out to smoke a joint and asked me if I wanted to come along. I said that I didn't smoke anymore, but that I would go along and keep them company.

"We got out behind this dumpster and they lit up and I knew I shouldn't be there. I said, 'I'm sorry, but I gotta go. I gotta get outta here.' They looked at me kind of weird, but they understood, and I headed out as fast as I could.

"I never thought I would be so happy to be back in treatment. After that experience, I knew that I wasn't ready to handle some things yet."

As Bob learned, it's best to do as the slogan says, Easy Does It and not put yourself into using situations until you're feeling pretty secure in your program. Also, if you're out on a weekend pass, make sure to attend AA or NA.

So What Does All This Get Me?

The Nuts and Bolts of Treatment

In most treatment programs, you'll work through at least the first three and, often, the first five Steps of the AA or NA program. These are:

Step One:

We admitted that we were powerless over alcohol [or "our addiction"] — that our lives had become unmanageable.

Step Two:

Came to believe that a Power greater than ourselves could restore us to sanity.

Step Three:

Made a decision to turn our will and our lives over to the care of God *as we understood Him.*

Step Four:

Made a searching and fearless moral inventory of ourselves.

Step Five:

Admitted to God, to ourselves, and to another human being the exact nature of our wrongs.

It's important, in working through the first five Steps, to define your Higher Power and experience and understand why having a Power greater than yourself is vital support on your path of sobriety. You'll take a good look at yourself and begin to discover what you like and dislike about yourself, and most important, you'll start learning to accept who you are.

Ideally, you'll get a good introduction to the remaining Steps and be able to apply them in your daily life. When you leave treatment and continue recovery, you'll also have begun to learn the importance of good communication with your family and peers. In the process, you'll be able to identify and express your feelings in a healthy manner.

You'll learn some of the skills necessary to deal with situations that trigger your urge to use, so you can handle them and avoid relapse. You'll also build a support system for yourself with the people in treatment and in AA or NA.

Finally, you'll have an opportunity to work on personal issues such as low self-esteem, abuse, and sexuality.

Some Additional Tips

1. If you're allowed to make phone calls, it's probably best not to call home a lot or talk to old friends (especially if they're using) on the outside when you're in treatment. They may have no idea what you're going through and it may be hard for them to be sympathetic. For now, focus on the people in treatment as you learn new communication and build new support systems.

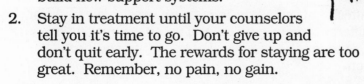

2. Stay in treatment until your counselors tell you it's time to go. Don't give up and don't quit early. The rewards for staying are too great. Remember, no pain, no gain.

3. Whether you're in an outpatient or coed inpatient setting, it's really important not to complicate your life with romantic involvement or sexual activity. Some experienced recovering addicts recommend at least six months before trying to get into a romantic relationship.

4. Toward the middle of treatment might be a good time to start looking for an AA or NA sponsor to help you through the tough transition to the outside.

You Mean There's an End to This?

What Happens When You Leave?

In inpatient treatment, when it's time for you to leave and if you're going home, you'll probably meet with staff and your family. During this meeting, you'll discuss your goals for school, job, family commitments, and so on.

If your home environment is not healthy or stable, you may be referred to a foster home, group home, or halfway house after treatment. This is especially true if your parents did not get involved in your chemical dependency treatment or if they're actively chemically dependent themselves.

Once you are out, you'll probably have some follow-up treatment or aftercare. This is often a group that meets once or twice a week for anywhere from four to sixteen weeks or longer. This group is a place where you can get support for the problems you're encountering as you continue to work on yourself.

You'll also want to attend AA or NA or another Twelve Step support group on a regular basis (see Chapter 3). You might want to check out your school for groups; many have a variety of support groups during or after school.

After treatment, you may be referred to a counselor or a different treatment center if you have specific personal, emotional, or family problems that you need to work on.

Testifying

Some People Who Should Know

Here are a few comments from some chemical dependency counselors about treatment.

Jim Heaslip, Manager of Residential Treatment at the Hazelden Pioneer House in Minneapolis, Minnesota:

Treatment is a small part of an individual's recovery. What they do when they leave treatment will be the major part of their recovery.

Nancy Wasberg, Chemical Dependency Counselor at the Freeway Unit for Chemical Dependency Treatment in Fergus Falls, Minnesota:

Little seeds are planted here. Whether those seeds grow·or not is up to the individual.

Jane Pavkovich, Chemical Dependency Counselor at the Alcohol and Chemical Dependency Unit of St. Cloud Hospital, St. Cloud, Minnesota:

. . . I'm not capable of changing people. That, they must do themselves.

I'm here to perhaps give people a reflection of how they're functioning, to promote growth, and to give them some feedback, but I'm not here to make changes in them. I care about people and I love them, but I'm not capable of changing them. That, they must do themselves.

Beth:

"When I went to treatment, I thought the only people there would be a bunch of hard-core bikers. I thought I'd get the shit beat out of me. By the time I was there an hour, I knew I was wrong. I started talking to the people and I found out they were really cool.

"The hardest part for me in treatment was realizing how bad I had treated my parents. They had always been so nice to me and I had always been such a bitch to them. It was hard to forgive myself for my behavior."

Jim:

"I thought treatment was going to be a break from life. I thought when I got out, I'd start drinking again, right away. . . . The hardest thing about treatment for me was dealing with my past, having to look back on my life. . . . I went through treatment twice. The first time I went through, I stayed straight for a while, but I don't think I realized how serious a problem I had. The second time, everything really sunk in."

Heather:

"I thought treatment would be a good place to meet guys. I also thought I would sail right through it.

"My first three days there, I was just like a total zombie. I had to be lead around to each activity. A using friend of mine was up there at the same time I was. Hearing him say he had a drug problem really opened my eyes, because I knew he used drugs the same way and the same amount as I did.

"Treatment opened my eyes to the tools I need to stay straight and how to have real friends and how to deal with problems without medicating.

"Treatment was hell! It was positive and helpful in the end, but definitely hell!"

Kari:

"I started drinking when I was twelve and started using other drugs shortly after that. When I made the switch from sixth grade to junior high school, I wanted to be popular and have people like me. It just seemed like anyone who was popular, used, so I started using. I used most of the common drugs, you know, booze, pot, speed, and coke.

"My grades dropped and I got high every day. My friends thought I was cool, you know, like really down to earth, but my self-esteem was the worst! I didn't like me at all. I felt like no matter what I did, nothing was really going to work out. I was just so tired of trying.

"I had it all planned out. I wanted to live until my sixteenth birthday and then I wanted to die. I was going to commit suicide. I had it planned so I would be successful too. I mean, I didn't want anybody finding me too soon and putting me in a mental ward or something. My sixteenth birthday was on a Monday and it would've worked out perfect with my parents' work schedules.

"Three days before my sixteenth birthday, my mom and dad picked me up at a friend's house and said, 'We've read your journal and we know all about your drug use and your sexual activity and we're taking you to treatment.'

"I knew that if I didn't go along with them, they'd probably never let me out of the house again! I knew that if I could go to the treatment center for their evaluation period and then get out, my parents would trust me.

"I didn't do very well in treatment. I went on a head trip with everything instead of getting at gut

23

feelings. Looking back now, I know I was bullshitting all the way through my evaluation. I told the staff I was really motivated to go straight. When the time came for my staff meeting, it was decided that I would attend outpatient treatment.

"Three weeks into my treatment, I had a slip. I think I had the slip because I didn't really open up to anybody, you know. I didn't feel like I fit in with my group at treatment, because they were all inpatient, but I didn't really fit in with my using friends either.

"After my slip, I continued the outpatient program and finished. By the time I finished the program, I had dealt with a lot of the negative emotions I was feeling.

"I know now that I'm chemically dependent, and I've been straight for ten months. My sobriety is really important to me."

Brandon:

"Treatment was the greatest experience of my life. I think everybody should go through it!"

Vickie:

"I had heard stories about treatment before I went in. I heard that they gave you shock treatments and brainwashed you. I wasn't very eager to go. Once I got there, I found out that none of it was true.

"I had a hard time being honest while I was there. I wanted everyone to like me. I'm a real people-pleaser, so I said what I thought they wanted to hear. I got a lot more out of treatment once I realized that I needed to be real.

"The worst part was facing my parents. I had been really selfish in the past because of my use. One time, my mom asked me to stay home on the weekend, because her sister was dying of cancer, and I said, 'No way. I got plans. We got a keg going.' I just cringe when I think of that. When you face it, though, you can deal with it."

Teresa:

(Excerpts from her journal while she was in treatment.)

May 21 — Today I feel angry and resentful. I guess that's normal though, 'cause that's usually the way I feel. People don't know it, though, 'cause I'm always smiling and joking around. I also don't trust anybody. I used to be real paranoid about that, but I guess it's just a defense.

May 27 — Today I sort of want to go to graduation. I asked for a pass. I feel angry today, but hopeful. I want to go straight, and if I apply the tools I've learned, I can do it, but these times when I'm so angry, the anger just kind of controls me and I know if I don't learn to deal with it, I'll go back to using.

Dean:

"If I can make it through treatment, anyone can! I was there against my will, and I had defenses stronger than a brick wall, and my family life was the pits. I don't think I even took the First Step till about halfway through.

"The one thing that will make you successful in treatment is to just shut up and feel what's in your gut. Deal with it, it's not going to go away. Do it now."

Tammy:

> "Treatment gives hope — belief that there's something better, there's something more to life than survival.

> "If I didn't go through treatment, I wouldn't be straight."

When you first come into treatment, it's easy to put your defenses up and try not to feel anything. But when you start to take down the barriers and allow yourself to feel the pain you're carrying around, the reward will be there.

Treatment is not a place where you go to escape your problems. It's a place where you confront them and learn to deal with them.

The people there won't judge you or think any less of you if they find out that you actually have a character defect or two. They are there to help you examine and accept yourself.

Don't be surprised if you have strong cravings and urges to use while you're in treatment. You're not strange; you just have a very powerful disease and this is part of your recovery — especially during the first few weeks.

Even if your body isn't in withdrawal anymore, part of your mind can still be convinced the only answer for *any* discomfort is drugs. That's the addict in you talking and your answer can be, "Not right now!"

Just tell yourself, *I won't use right now,* and try the following:

- I'll talk to my Higher Power.
- I'll talk to a friend or counselor.
- I'll read some program or other inspirational material.
- I'll sweat it out — run, swim, punch a bag, or do push-ups.
- I'll go help someone else in need.
- I'll distract myself — cards, a puzzle, a painting, a tape.

Be sure you don't hide your feelings and try to handle everything alone. Take it to your next group or individual counseling session. *Talk* about it — don't let your addict shame you.

Remember, One Day at a Time can sometimes mean one hour or even one minute at a time, but you can make it through this without using.

Treatment will not *cure* you. Chemical dependency is an incurable disease, but it *is* treatable. Treatment can teach you how, through abstinence and working a program, you can lead a normal, comfortable, and even exciting life, clean and sober.

. . . don't hide your feelings and try to handle everything alone.

Life After Treatment, *Or* Am I Well Yet?

The Other 95 Percent

Doug was one of my favorite people while I was in treatment. He was always cracking jokes. I think we were especially close because I used to party with him when we were still using, and we could see how far each other had come.

One day, he pulled me aside after lunch and said, "Guess what? I get out tomorrow."

"Tomorrow?" I responded, "Wow! Great!"

"Yep. They're springin' me. I'll be a free man."

"Well, that's great, Doug. Congratulations!"

"You see, Dana," he went on, "I'm well now. I'm fixed. I'm cured. . . ." He was on a roll now. Once Doug got started, there was no stopping him. "Yeah, that's it, cured. One hundred and fifty-nine easy counseling sessions and you too can be cured of this dreaded disease. Yes it truly is a miracle, ladies and gentlemen."

"Doug, you are so weird."

Then he leaned over and whispered in my ear. "Just between you and me, I don't feel well yet. I mean, I still feel sick, but don't tell anyone. They might change their mind."

Doug got me thinking. I started wondering, *What does it mean to be well?* and *Where do we go from here?*

The whole time I was in treatment, I thought about getting out and how great it would be to have a normal life. As the event crept closer, however, I started to get worried.

I had heard all the sayings. You know, like "Treatment is only 5 percent of recovery. It gives you the tools you need, and the other 95 percent of recovery is putting those tools to use." Well, what if I didn't get it right? I mean, what if I picked up a screwdriver and I should have grabbed a hammer? The prospect of *never* being "well" was pretty depressing, but all of a sudden the prospect of going into the real world seemed even worse.

It occurred to me that I was terrified to leave treatment. I couldn't believe it. All that I had thought about for the past month was getting out and now I was scared.

. . . I was terrified to leave treatment.

I could live with the fact that I wasn't going to be "cured." After all, there were people out there with other diseases like epilepsy and diabetes who lived relatively normal lives without being cured, so why couldn't I? What I really wanted to know was how it was going to be to live my life clean and sober. Was there life after treatment?

The purpose of this chapter is to give you some idea of what to expect out in the "real world." I'll talk about some of the obstacles you'll encounter and some of the options you have.

The Halfway House

Many of you, when you leave treatment, will move back home. But since this is not possible for all people, let's take a minute to talk about halfway houses.

Some people have a difficult time going directly back home or out on their own after treatment. For some, home may be an abusive environment or maybe just not a supportive one. Others may depend too much on their family and need to become more independent. Perhaps, to maintain their sobriety, they need a controlled environment for a while. There are many reasons why someone would not be comfortable in their old home environment. Whatever the reason, it's important that an extra burden not be put unnecessarily on anyone's recovery. This is where halfway houses come in.

For many, a halfway house really is halfway between treatment and home. It's a goal for all chemically dependent people to eventually live comfortably on their own. The halfway house can be a stepping-stone.

In a halfway house, you live with other recovering addicts, most of whom have also been in treatment and are often close in age. Some halfway houses are coed (both sexes living together) and some are strictly male or female. There is usually at least one adult living in the home who supervises activities.

If you're still in school, you're encouraged to attend regularly, in addition to working a job or doing some kind of volunteer work in the community. These activities give you an opportunity to gradually test your new sobriety.

You will also have chores or responsibilities at the halfway house. Every person at the house is supposed to pitch in and do his or her share. These chores can be anything from setting the table or mowing the lawn, to making meals or doing laundry.

Often, you'll have an opportunity to talk to a counselor, if not at the halfway house, then at a local mental health facility or treatment center. In the halfway house, there are usually Alcoholics Anonymous meetings and other support groups scheduled. These help you continue to work on yourself and deal with the problems you are having, and you get to know the people you're living with better. You are also encouraged to attend AA or NA meetings outside of the house.

A stay at a halfway house can last from three to twelve months or longer. Ideally, young people eventually end up back home or living on their own. But if this isn't possible, a foster home or other more permanent supportive living arrangement can be found.

Halfway houses are not for everyone, but for many the time spent there is an important transition in their long-term recovery.

. . . getting to know others better.

Life in the Real World

Re-entry

So it's time for you to leave the halfway house. Or maybe you're going back into the world right out of treatment. Let's talk a little about reentry into your old environment, then we'll go into some detail about some obstacles you may encounter.

Maybe you're thinking, *Geez, You're making being straight sound so hard. I mean, all this talk about obstacles. It sounds like a lot of work.*

At first, when you're off alcohol or other drugs, there are usually some areas of your life or character defects that you may need to work on. It's up to you when and where you do it. Some people who are right out of treatment just go into seclusion for a while and avoid confronting others — and that isn't necessarily bad. People need to decide for themselves what works for them and when they need to do things. Most of us do put forth the effort and work on ourselves, just because we've learned the hard way that we'll get more out of life by putting something into it.

Todd:

(A twenty-one-year-old who loves basketball and has two years' sobriety.)

"It probably doesn't sound very healthy, but when I first got home, other than AA meetings,

33

I basically kind of hibernated. I spent a lot of time at home, reading and spending time with my family. I read the whole Big Book, cover to cover — no kidding! I just needed that time to myself. It worked out well for me. By the time I became part of civilization again, I felt more comfortable with my sobriety."

Lindsey:

(A seventeen-year-old computer whiz who has been in recovery for six months.)

"I just jumped back into everything when I got out. I guess I figured that I would have to face the world sometime and it would be better to meet situations head-on. I spent a lot of time with straight people and kept the rest of my life pretty much the same; although I didn't and still don't set myself up. I mean, I don't go to using parties or anything."

What amazes most people about being straight is not how hard it is, but how much easier it is than they thought it would be. When we're using, we can't even imagine being straight, much less liking it. It's amazing how easy the transition can be when you hang around with the right people and take care of yourself.

Like any new lifestyle, though, there will be situations that are new and it sometimes helps to think about them ahead of time to prepare ourselves. So let's get to it.

Going Back to School

One thing to keep in mind as you encounter these new situations is that, although you may feel that you have changed and grown a lot as a result of treatment, the rest of the world doesn't know this yet. Not only that, the rest of the world has probably stayed pretty much the same while you were gone.

On the chalkboard: ALAMO / TITANIC / WATE

There's a strong possibility that you weren't a model student. . . .

For one thing, when you go back to school, chances are your teachers and other school officials aren't going to throw you a welcome back party. Don't get me wrong, there are some who have a good understanding of addiction and who will be supportive (hopefully this group is growing every day), but the majority of school administrators and teachers will carry on as though you never left.

Don't take these reactions personally. It may be that they've seen more than one student complete treatment and go back to using. They may want to see where you're at. And let's face it — there's a strong possibility that you weren't a "model" student before you left, so they may need time adjusting to the new you.

Jack:

(An eighteen-year-old who had a hard-core reputation while using.)

"The best thing I ever did is a few days before I was due back in school, I made an appointment with my school guidance counselor. I went to school early, you know, before any of the other kids were there. I talked to the counselor and let her know that I just finished treatment and I was going to stay straight. I told her I was going to AA and stuff like that. She was really cool about it and really interested. She asked me all about what it was like.

"It was really strange to be getting along with her so well, we'd had so many run-ins before. We both kind of looked at this like a fresh start.

"After I was done talking to her, I went around to each of my teachers and talked to them for a few minutes to let them know I was back and when I would be back in class, that kind of thing.

"This whole process was really weird for me. I mean, I kept thinking, *I can't believe I'm acting this way. I mean this is just too straight,* but I'm glad I did it. It's probably the first time in my life I acted responsibly, and it made it easier to mentally get into my classes again."

If you didn't like school before you were in treatment, just because you're straight doesn't mean you're going to love it now, but it doesn't mean you'll hate it either.
Living a clean and sober life means having choices. You may still dislike certain subjects, but now you can choose to make the best of things. In treatment you

learned coping skills — how to deal with difficult people and situations rather than running away. School is just one area to test your wings.

The Old Gang

Going sober doesn't necessarily mean that you'll want to hang out with a completely different group of people. Being straight doesn't mean becoming somebody you're not. If you dress a certain way, talk a certain way, or have a certain image, that's okay — you may or may not stick with it. The same holds true for using friends. You may or may not want to hang out with them after going straight. You may not be sure of how they'll treat you or what they'll think about you, and the thought of talking to them about being sober is probably intimidating.

One important thing to remember is that you will have a group of friends for support if you participate in AA or NA.

Teresa:

"When I was in treatment, I called one of my old using friends and told her where I was and that I had decided to go straight. I told her that I couldn't hang out with her anymore, because I couldn't handle being around using.

"She said that she totally understood and that she thought it was really cool that I was doing something to better myself. She also said maybe sometime we could go out and not use, you know, to a movie or something.

"I was shocked! I thought for sure she would hate me. I think if someone is going straight and they're worried about their using friends, they should realize that if these people are really your friends, they'll support you."

Heather:

"Four of my old using friends are straight now. It's so great! I never imagined I could be as close to anybody as I am to these friends."

Justin:

"When I see my using friends, they'll sometimes give me shit about being straight. But one thing I've learned: if you don't preach to your friends about their using, they won't bug you about your not using."

Renee:

"My using friends were afraid I'd try to talk them into going straight. I don't even see them anymore."

. . . if I talk about my feelings and things that aren't superficial, they can't really deal with it.

Kari:

"I think I am a major threat to my using friends. You know, they think that because I decided to go straight, then maybe they're using too much. I never say anything to them about their use, but I've noticed when I talk about my feelings and things that aren't superficial, they can't really deal with it."

Jim:

"I didn't see my using friends the whole time I was in treatment, so we just never started up contact again."

Nancy:

"When I was still using, my best friend, Mary, went straight. She told me she couldn't handle hanging out with me. I understood and kept using. Then, I started to think about my use. You know, if Mary's got a problem and we used the same way, maybe I've got a problem too.

"I started seeing changes in her for the better and things were getting worse and worse for me. Finally I asked her if I could go to AA with her — now I'm straight.

"I'm so glad Mary went straight, even though she didn't know how the rest of us who were still using would react."

When it comes to dealing with your friends who use, there are no easy answers. It really is an individual decision, but here are a few guidelines you can follow:

- *Respect where they're at with using.* Don't try to push your ideas about being straight on them. Your example is the best way to get through to them.
- *Don't get defensive or into name-calling sessions.* If someone calls you a "lightweight" or says you can't

handle it, say, "That's right, I can't!" It takes all the fun out of it when you agree with them.

- *Stay away from them when they're using, even if you think you can handle it.* Just explain that you can't be around them because it's too much of a temptation to use. Maybe they'll understand and be able to identify with that.
- *Have a good support group.* Don't expect your using friends to provide that for you. Go to AA or NA. Make friends with people who are straight.

Your using friends may respect you for being independent and for trying to be yourself. After all, they're friends, right?

Don't be surprised if you find yourself spending less and less time with them or maybe no time at all. As you develop straight friends, you won't have as much in common with people who use.

Special Relationships

Relationships can be difficult under any circumstances, but when one-half of a couple decides to make a major lifestyle change, it can get especially complicated.

Everybody's situation is different. Perhaps the best thing to do is to hear how some other people dealt with their relationships after going straight.

Joyce:

"My relationship with Jim was a disaster! We had been going out for two years before I went into treatment, so I was reluctant to just scrap it, but it just couldn't work.

"The whole time I was in treatment, he didn't come to groups, and he used pretty heavy. When I got out, we would spend time together and try to get to know each other again, but it was like we were from two different worlds. He was still really into

the party scene and I was into trying to grow up.
It didn't take long to figure out that it was over."

. . . it was like we were from two different worlds.

Cory:

"I hadn't been going out with Joan for very long
when I went into treatment. Joan drank, but she
was definitely what anybody would call a social
drinker. She came to all the family groups during
treatment and she goes to Al-Anon. She doesn't
drink anymore either, although she doesn't consider herself an alcoholic. She has just been great
through all of this, and the whole experience has
really helped us to grow together."

Sandy:

"I was straight for ten months before I met Greg. We met at an AA sponsored dance. He had six months' sobriety at the time. It was the first relationship for either of us since we'd been straight. We really had to take it one step at a time. We've been going out for seven months now and I'm sure it's the healthiest relationship that either of us has had."

Matt:

"Being straight doesn't guarantee a positive relationship. Patty and I went out together for a couple of months, but it just wasn't very positive. I was dealing with some major female dependency issues and she was dealing with some past abuse issues. We really weren't helping each other. We're still friends, but I need to just be on my own for a while."

The most important thing you can do when thinking about your relationship or the prospect of getting into one, is to ask yourself, *Is this healthy for me? Do I feel good with this person sober or do I feel like using again?* Or simply, *Are we helping one another or hurting one another?*

We'll cover relationships more fully in Chapter 6.

Going Back to a Job

Much of the same applies here as with going back to school and hanging out with using friends. Talk to your boss ahead of time about coming back. Remember, your co-workers may not have changed, even though you have. You may need to own up to some past behavior that was irresponsible or abusive. Apologies are nice but the only sure way to make up for the past is to stay straight One Day at a Time and do your work to the best of your ability — for yourself.

Anita:

> *(A sixteen-year-old who works in a fast-food restaurant.)*
>
> "I think if I had to do it over again, I would try to relax and be more honest with the people I work with. I think they would have understood if I just said, 'It's weird being back. I'm not sure how to act.' People can usually understand what it's like to be unsure of yourself."

You may run into some of the same problems with using friends at work as in school. Changing old patterns, like eating with a different group of co-workers instead of getting stoned on your breaks or after work, may take some getting used to. But it can also open up possibilities you've missed, like new friendships and the satisfaction of better job performance.

Your Parents and Family

Now that you're straight, you'll get along with your parents all the time, right? Well . . . not really. It may take some time for old wounds to heal and for all of you to unlearn old, destructive ways of relating to each other.

Even though you're straight, you may still act out (or they may still put you in) the same role you had in the family when you used. It takes time for a family to change.

And there's the chance things just won't change. Then, you'll have to make a choice between your recovery and staying in a situation that triggers your cravings for drugs.

At best, you'll probably still fight and they'll still put restrictions on you that you don't like. But these don't have to become excuses to use. Remember, if you use, you damage *your* life, not theirs.

Most young people say that when they went straight, their relationship with their parents improved greatly. Many said they began to see their parents as people and talked to them more like friends.

Hopefully, the main difference you'll notice in your confrontations is that now you can tell them how you really feel. You don't have to hold back your feelings because you're afraid to say what's really going on inside. Everybody's situation is a little different.

Jackie:

"My family is pretty messed up. My folks are divorced and both of them use heavy duty. It's really very hard for me sometimes. I watch the two of them self-destruct and it seems hopeless. It's really hard to remember that I can only take care of myself and not them.

"I go to a *lot* of meetings! Everything — AA, NA, Alateen, and Adult Children of Alcoholics. I have built up a good support system for myself, and I spend as much time as I can with my sister. She lives on her own and is involved with the program too.

"I know it's just a few more years and I'm outta here. I don't mean to sound grim, but I know I'm not going to live with them forever and I need to just work my program in the meantime and take it One Day at a Time."

Jason:

"Since I've been home, most everything has been going smooth. My parents and I get along better than ever and I've been able to get my life back on track. The only thing that has been a drag is that my brother is still using.

"We used to get high together and I'm sure he feels like I betrayed him. He thinks that the folks think I'm some kind of angel and he's the black sheep or something. I'm just not sure how to deal with it. I've talked to him and told him how I feel about his use and that I want us to be friends. I think that helped a little.

"It's especially hard, because I get the urge to get high when I smell weed coming from his room in the basement. Most of the time, I just get out of the house. It helps if I stay in touch with my Higher Power."

Chuck:

"My mom is so conservative it's unreal. She is still going through total denial about this whole thing. I can't talk to her about my use or about my being straight. She would die if I ever mentioned anything in front of anybody else. She has a lot of shame over the fact that I'm a drug addict. I need to be careful not to get on a big guilt trip and fall into a pity bag. The best thing I can do for myself is to be accepting — of me and her."

Toni:

"My mom and I are best friends. I know that's really cliché, but it's true. She's so supportive. I can't believe she's the same woman that I would fight with every day just a few months ago. I'm so thankful for my sobriety and that we had an opportunity to develop this friendship."

Most parents will automatically have more respect and trust in you when you go straight. They know that you are trying to take care of yourself.

When dealing with any family member, just remember that you can only take care of yourself and your own program. Do what it takes to stay straight.

More about authority figures later.

Don't Use: Go to Meetings

Using Situations

No matter what you do, you will encounter situations where the people around you will be using. There are weddings, job picnics, parties, rock concerts, and on and on. After all, you can't live in a bubble. These situations can go smoothly and you may even enjoy yourself.

If possible, arrange to have someone else who's straight there with you. It's always easier not to be the only one.

When someone asks you what you'd like to drink, just tell them "club soda" or whatever. You will be astonished that most people won't even think twice about that.

If somebody says, "Want a beer?" or "Aw come on, just one hit won't kill you!" or something to that effect, say, "No, thanks." You don't have to explain yourself or say why you aren't drinking or using. Most people really don't care.

Once in a while you'll run into the person who will ask you why you're not drinking or using. It's not that surprising when you consider that every time before this, he or she may have seen you getting loose. All you have to say is, "I just don't feel like drinking tonight" or, "I'm taking it easy today" (after all, you are only straight for twenty-four hours at a time). You don't have to tell someone that you're alcoholic or a drug addict if you're uncomfortable with that or if you don't want to get into it.

If they keep at you, you may decide to tell them you're an alcoholic or addict. Don't be surprised if they drop the subject after that (or else give you a history of how they "only drink a couple of beers on weekends").

The main thing to remember is that most people won't think it's strange you don't drink or use other drugs, especially if you feel okay with it.

And don't be afraid to leave an event early if you can't handle it. No one will probably see it as a big deal anyway.

Now for a few "war" stories from other young people's experiences.

Mark:

> "At our employee Christmas party there always was a lot of drinking. I dreaded the thought of going. I really built it up in my mind that it would be a horrible experience, but it wasn't bad at all. No one there seemed to care that I wasn't getting

loaded. I danced and talked to everyone. My boss's husband even came up to me and said that he heard I was straight and he thought it was really 'admirable' that I could do that in today's society."

LeAnn:

"I went to a family reunion this past summer and I have mixed feelings about it. I had a hard time with some of my uncles and cousins — the ones that use heavy and that I used to drink with. They gave me a rough time about not being able to handle my liquor and things like that, but then there was this other side to it that was a whole new experience for me. I never realized it, but there are a lot of people in my family who *are* straight! I couldn't help but wonder how long these people have been at reunions and I was always too busy getting wasted to notice. It was neat to meet them and to know that now at the next wedding, shower, or anniversary, there will be people there who are straight like I am."

Ron:

"For a long time after I went straight, I didn't go to parties where people were using. When I went to my first one, I was scared to death. I don't know what made me want to go, but it was one of the typical summer ones with a bonfire and that kind of thing. I decided that if I was going to go, I was going to have a good time and I was going to be prepared, because my sobriety was too important to me to blow it.

"First, I went out and bought a cooler full of different kinds of mineral waters and other nonalcoholic drinks. I figured variety would make it easier. It's crazy, but everyone else was drinking my stuff. It was kind of neat that my being there gave them a choice.

"Next, I had an AA friend who knew some of the same people I did, come with me. Maybe it sounds paranoid, but I wouldn't want to have gone alone.

"I think the best thing was that while I was there, I didn't spend a lot of time talking to just one person. I spread out and talked to everyone. It was great! It worked out well for me because I didn't leave wishing that I could do it every weekend or wishing that I was using again. I took it for what it was, fun for one night.

"Since that first time, I've had some bad experiences at parties where there was using, but I think the key was knowing when it was time to leave."

Urges

When you go straight, there may be times when it feels like you can't stop thinking about using and your urges or cravings seem really powerful. This is completely normal, and most of us have found that the longer we're straight, the less it will happen.

The first six months to a year can be especially hard.

Depending on which drugs and how much of them you used, it may take you a year or longer just to start thinking and feeling normal again.

No matter how often or

how strong the urge to use is, you have a choice now as to what you do about it.

When you are newly straight, it is best to avoid putting yourself in situations where you used to use, and just stay away from parties and bars completely. If you always used when you went to a ball game, then avoid the stress of ball games until you're ready to handle it. Or at least make sure you go with people who don't use and know you're straight.

Kari:

"Using is really not an option for me. I know things will not get better if I use, only worse.

"When I get the urge to use, sometimes I go inward, you know, turn off the lights in my room and meditate. Sometimes I need to call someone from AA. A guy I know from AA, Sid — I called him the other night at 2:30 A.M. If you want to stay straight bad enough, you'll do what it takes."

Teresa:

"I think it through, you know, what would *really* happen if I used. I talk about it in AA too."

Heather:

"I like to think, *How do I live happier?* not *How do I stay straight?* That means I don't even consider using. When I use, I'm suicidal. If I get the urge, I call someone."

Brian:

"I very seldom get the urge to use anymore. When I do, I just think to myself, *It's not worth it, I'll just feel worse, not better.*"

Dennis:

"I just remind myself that I'm not going to use today. If I have to, I take it minute by minute and try to concentrate on something else."

Tammy:

"I call someone straight or I talk to my mom. If it's really late, I'll write in my journal."

Renee:

"I remember the depression I had when I used. I grow more and more the longer I'm straight."

Mitch:

"I have to think it through, step by step. First, *How is it going to feel?* Then, *What will I do or say that is embarrassing?* Then, *How will I feel when it's over?* And so on. By the time I'm done with that, I've usually come to my senses. If not, I call my sponsor right away."

Beth:

"I've had slips before, when I've gone back to using. When I get the urge to use now, I think about how bad I feel when I had slips before. I just think about how much fun I have when I'm straight, and then I call someone straight."

Jim:

"I usually just think it through. I think about the negative things about using . . . and I talk about it at meetings."

Along with the urge to use, your mind may play tricks on you. You may catch yourself thinking, *I could have just one drink or hit.* The best way to avoid this stinkin' thinkin' is to go to lots of AA or NA meetings and stay around sober people.

You Mean They're Really Not a Bunch Of Winos?
Or
Some Facts About Twelve Step Meetings

A Quiz

All right, what's the first image that comes to mind when you hear the words, "Alcoholics Anonymous"? Circle one.

A.   A group of hard-core drunks, sitting around smoking filterless cigarettes, drinking day-old coffee, telling endless drunk stories.

B.   A man or woman who is ragged, terrified, and looks like he or she hasn't slept for about a month, standing in front of a group, saying, "I'm _____, and I'm an alcoholic" and then going into a fourteen-hour speech on how he or she hit bottom.

C.   All of the above.

Well, let's just say that those images are slightly outdated.

Okay, So, What Is AA Like? How About a Few Concrete Facts?

- AA was founded by two men, Bill W. and Dr. Bob[1] back in 1935. Both men had hit bottom and they founded AA with the concept that the best person to help an alcoholic is someone who has been in the same situation — one drunk helping another.
- The members of AA are recovering alcoholics who go to AA for the support of fellow members in order to keep straight. They're not a bunch of prudes who preach about the "evils of liquor."
- AA is self-supporting, with no fees or dues, and operates only on donations from members.
- AA is for both sexes, all ages, races, religions, economic, and social backgrounds. *The Twelve Steps and Twelve Traditions* says, "The only requirement for membership is a desire to stop drinking." If you want, you can often find AA groups specifically for women, men, gays, lesbians, young people, or older people. People who have a problem with alcohol and other drugs are welcome and often outnumber the "pure" alcoholics. But at AA the emphasis is on the drug alcohol.
- AA members are there to talk about *their* drinking and *their* lives of recovery, not to judge you, your past use, or how you stay sober.

AA members are not there to judge you . . .

---

[1] Anonymity has been practiced by AA members since it was founded; thus no last names are required.

- There are AA chapters in just about every city and town in the U.S., and hundreds worldwide. You can usually find a meeting practically any day of the week and nearly any time of day in large cities, and usually at least one meeting a week in small towns.

What's in It for Me?

Now you may be thinking, *Well, no offense, but that all sounds very boring. What's in it for me? Why should I go to a Twelve Step meeting like AA?*

For one thing it works. AA offers a plan of action that can help anyone go straight, and, from its beginning, it has proven to be the most successful way around to stay straight.[2] Most alcoholics, other addicts, and addiction professionals will tell you it's just plain necessary if you really don't want to use again, but another very important reason to go to AA meetings is to meet and make friends with other straight people your own age.

Julianne:

"When I talk to people who are thinking about going straight or who are just in treatment, they always say something like, 'AA sounds great, but I already have a group of people that I hang around with. They may drink, but they're my friends, and I don't want to start hanging out with a whole new group.'

"I just let them know that I'm not saying they have to give up their using friends. You know, maybe they're comfortable being straight around friends who still use. Or maybe they'll decide to be around them only when they're not using. All's I'm saying is that recovering people probably won't be straight for long if they feel like they're the only one. When they go to AA or NA, it gives them an opportunity to talk to other straight people who

---

[2] Narcotics Anonymous and other Twelve Step programs would apply here, and to this entire chapter, since the Twelve Steps and Twelve Traditions originating with AA are the foundation of other Twelve Step programs.

are going through the same thing that they are. They're going to think being straight is a drag if everyone around them is drinking or using.

"I tell people to check out AA, see how they like it. Try different meetings and you never know — most people find out that the more time they spend with straight people, the less they want to see of their using friends."

Brian:

"AA is a meeting place. We go to straight parties after the meeting, or sometimes straight dances sponsored by AA."

Beth:

"I don't talk much at the meetings. I get a lot out of listening, especially to members who've been going for a long time. We're like a family."

Nancy:

"I hated my first AA meeting. I was scared to death to go. The room was so smoky and there were no young people there. It was awful!

"I'm really glad I kept going, though, and checked out other meetings. I eventually met a bunch of people my own age. A whole group of us gets together sometimes to take road trips to AA meetings in other towns and go out afterward."

Jim:

"When I'm feeling really down, I can go and talk at meetings and get it out."

Karen:

"When I first went to AA, I thought *Wow, these people have fun and they don't drink! You're kidding!* Now I just like the support and I adore the people, even those I don't know very well."

Teresa:

"AA is so fun! It's just fun to be with straight people. You can apply the situations of other people to your own life."

Heather:

"AA is friendships. That's my meaning for AA, and the friendships are not fake — they're real true friendships. I can say what I feel at AA and not worry if I make sense or if anyone is going to judge me. I can be totally open. No matter what you say, do, or are, you're okay."

Josh:

"I just freaked out when I went to my first AA meeting. It was a Young People's meeting and it was on a Saturday night. Now I don't live in a very big city, you know, we're just average size, but there were a hundred people there! I couldn't believe it. I never expected that."

Jerry:

"I was really paranoid about going to my first meeting. I thought everyone there would be the burnout type and I just didn't think I would fit in. I didn't think they would accept me. What was crazy, there were people from every walk of life. Any type of person you could imagine. It wasn't cliquey either. I mean, it's weird, but it's the only place I've ever seen a punker, a jock, a prep, and a biker all hang out together!"

AA is not just a program, it's a place to make friends. Not only friends that you share your feelings with, but friends that you can "party" with too.

AA is definitely not the only entertainment there is when you're straight, but it's a great starting point.

How AA Can Help You Stay Straight

Each person in AA has the freedom and flexibility to work out a way of life that is best for him or her. AA does offer suggestions and guidelines that make the road of sobriety a little easier.

The first thing you'll learn about being straight is you can only do it One Day at a Time. Most of us can't imagine *never taking another drink* or *not using drugs for the rest of our life.* Forever is too long for anyone to manage; however, we can handle staying straight for twenty-four hours.

Some members say that if they get the urge to drink they just take it one hour at a time. There may even be times when it's minute by minute. Usually, though, a day at a time works fine.

Hardly anyone would like to think about not drinking or using other drugs for the rest of his or her life.

The Twelve Step Program

The AA program consists of Twelve Steps that are kind of a road map for sobriety. Bill W. and the first AA members didn't set them up as a code of behavior or a set of rules we have to swear by.

If you completed some kind of treatment program, you have probably gone over Steps One through Five thoroughly and know something about the other seven.

Every person eventually has his or her own interpretation of what each Step means. The definitions that follow are my own and are not endorsed by AA in any way. As you talk to members of AA and go to Step meetings (AA meetings where each week a Step is introduced and discussed by the group), you'll hear many different interpretations. Your own experience with each Step will change, too, as you grow in the program.

Step One:

> We admitted we were powerless over alcohol [or "our addiction"]— that our lives had become unmanageable.

Step One, in the simplest terms is saying, "We know now we are alcoholics. Once we start drinking (or using), we cannot control how much we will use (powerlessness), in spite of the great harm that alcohol and other drugs continue to cause in our life (unmanageability)."

Joey:

> *(A twenty-year-old who had a lot of denial to break through in order to take the First Step, and who now has a year and a half of sobriety.)*

> "The First Step was so hard for me. The first problem I had was that I was raised in an abusive family. I think it's because of this that I had such a temper and was really violent. It was really bad when I was using. I always had this really macho concept of power. You know, I was in control. Well, anyway, I ended up in treatment and they wanted me to say I'm powerless! No way. I call the shots!

> "The more I got into the program, the more I realized that my drinking — my alcoholism — is a disease. I had to ask myself, 'Does the kid with leukemia have the power to change that?' I mean, I'm lucky. My disease is treatable and I can work the program and stay sober, today, but I am definitely powerless. I need to accept that this is life and death I'm dealing with here, and there's no room for my power trip, and I had to get help for my violence too.

"As far as unmanageability, I probably wouldn't have figured out that I had a problem in the first place if my life wasn't caving in from all ends. I probably would still be rationalizing and denying everything."

What Joey experienced and what we all have to experience in our own way, is hitting bottom. This is when we don't *think* we're powerless over booze, we *know* it!

Step Two:

Came to believe that a Power greater than ourselves could restore us to sanity.

Step Two talks about the insanity caused by our drinking and how continuing to drink and use other drugs, even though they are causing problems in many areas of our life, is crazy behavior.

In order for our life to be normal (sane) again, this Step suggests that it's necessary to have a belief in a "Higher Power." Now, AA is *not* a religion. You do not have to give up all worldly pleasures or start preaching in the streets in order to have a belief in a Higher Power. You only need to work out what or who your "Higher Power" is. Some members consider a "Power greater than ourselves" to be the AA group itself. For others, their Higher Power is more personal and is directly involved in their lives. For still others, a Higher Power may be a peaceful force that binds all life together such as Nature or Creation. It's up to each of us, but what's

You don't have to give up all worldly pleasures . . .

important to remember is that our willpower cannot keep us straight anymore; only a Power greater than ourselves can make our life normal again.

Jessie:

(A nineteen-year-old raised in a fairly strict Catholic family who has ten months of sobriety.)

"The whole time I was drinking, I totally got away from my church and belief in any kind of God or anything — except maybe when I was in trouble and would do my usual 'bargain' prayers. The main reason I had a problem with spirituality as I knew it was because it seemed so unreal, you know, like there was some old white-haired man watching over us all. That was just too much like Santa Claus for me to take seriously!

"Well anyway, I was raised in a church system that was very male dominated and very old-fashioned and I was bummed out to think that I wasn't going to be able to stay sober unless I went back to that old white-haired-man-in-a-robe theory. Then I figured out that a Higher Power is what *I* interpret it to be.

"I believe and always believed that there is kind of a 'glue' that holds us all together. You know, the love and good in each human being — the emotion, the force that holds us all together. Maybe it's just a collective spirit, but it's definitely something very positive. The word *higher* is probably not accurate for me, it's more like *within*. Anyway, I do feel that I can pray and make a positive connection with this energy and it will make my life better.

"I don't know, maybe the old-timers in AA would freak out if they knew how I felt about my Higher Power. They would probably think I'm totally distorted, but it works for me.[3] I just don't think

---

[3] Actually, the old-timers went through very much the same struggle Jessie did, and many came to have a similar experience with their Higher Power.

most people my age like to think of their Higher Power as kind of a 'ultimately high, authority figure.'

"My Higher Power is so important to my sobriety because now I never feel alone, and I also feel that I am an important part of this universe. It makes a difference. I feel more at peace."

Step Three:

Made a decision to turn our will and our lives over to the care of God *as we understood Him.*

Step Three is about making a decision to live our life spiritually instead of obsessed with self-centeredness. It's talking about being willing to have faith and accept the situations that our life will bring, knowing that everything happens for a reason.

Mary Kay:

(A twenty-one-year-old recovering alcoholic who would like to become a high school math teacher.)

"When I was using and I'd get angry or upset or depressed or just stressed out with emotion, I'd get loaded or high. I used to get really hyper when I couldn't control things around me. I just couldn't deal with it and I'd get into a lot of game playing.

"Turning it over — turning my will and life over to my Higher Power — means being willing to just say 'Hey, I can't handle this and I'm not going to deal with it anymore. I just need your help, God. You're going to have to take care of this one.'

"I swear it works! If I am willing to just trust and go on with my life, I don't need to control every little thing in my life. I don't have to stress out and use. I don't have to put up with crappy situations either. Instead, I just turn it over and focus my energies on things that I can change, you know, 'the wisdom to know the difference.'"[4]

Step Four:

Made a searching and fearless moral inventory of ourselves.

What is meant by an "inventory" in Step Four is not only listing all the things we did when we were using that were harmful to ourselves or others. It's also about taking a good look at our personality and being honest about the traits we like in ourselves and those we dislike. It's not often in life that people have the opportunity to do this, and if we can examine ourselves completely and honestly, it's possible to make some fantastic changes.

The goal here is not to punish ourselves or to try to be perfect, but to accept ourselves as we are. If we know our character defects, we can be aware when they surface in our dealings with other people. And if we know our positive traits, we can build on those traits to live a fuller life that shows our real values.

Made a searching and fearless moral inventory of ourselves.

Here are some common character defects and their flip side positive traits that people in the program have found. Look at them and write down on a separate sheet of paper how they've affected your life.

- *Perfectionism* — setting unreal standards for yourself and then being frustrated if you don't meet them. It also means not being able to accept flaws in others.
- **Accepting imperfection** — being able to admit and accept that you're human.

64

---

[4] This refers to the Serenity Prayer often used to open or close meetings.

- *False pride, vanity, selfishness* — being so thin-skinned that you have trouble admitting any human weakness at all, and feeling as if you have to look good for others, even if that means making other people look bad.
- **Humility, modesty, unselfishness** — being humble doesn't mean being weak. It means accepting yourself — your strengths as well as your weaknesses, and expecting others to accept you as you are.

- *Greed, unkindness, excessiveness* — doing whatever it takes to satisfy your own needs, even if it hurts others.
- **Generosity, kindness, modesty** — caring enough about others to be able to respond to their needs.

- *Impatience, intolerance, narrow-mindedness, sarcastic* — wanting something now, cutting down other points of view, and acting as if your way is the only right way.
- **Patience, tolerance, open-mindedness, supportiveness** — taking it easy, taking things as they come, and not feeling as if you have to control everything.

- *Self-pity, hopelessness, pessimism, self-hatred, cowardice* — feeling sorry for yourself. Feeling that people don't understand, respect, or love you enough. Feeling like no one has it as bad as you do.
- **Self-respect, hopefulness, optimism, self-love, courage** — respecting yourself and feeling worthwhile. Knowing that you are capable, can take action, and will work things out.

- *Resentment, vengefulness, bitterness* — hanging on to angry feelings.
- **Compassion, forgiveness, peacefulness** — understanding and accepting those who've wronged you.

- *Dishonesty, lying, manipulating* — justifying your behavior; lying to others and yourself. Doing anything to get what you want.
- **Honesty, truthfulness, sincerity** — being open about how you feel, what you've done, and accepting the consequences — both the good and the bad.

- *Envy, jealousy, suspicion* — not wanting to see others have what you don't have. Thinking you have to have the best all the time.
- **Graciousness, goodwill, trusting** — being happy for those around you and liking yourself for who you are.

- *Procrastination, avoidance, irresponsibility, sloppiness* — waiting till the last minute to take care of things or not doing them at all. Complaining about your circumstances.
- **Energy, enterprise, responsibility, spirit** — meeting things head-on and caring enough to do what needs to be done.

- *Promiscuity, infidelity, sexual abusiveness, self-gratification, disrespect* — not caring about the people you are sexually involved with.
- **Restraint, faithfulness, decency, considerate, respectfulness** — upholding your personal sexual values and other values in relationships.

- *Guilt, shame* — feeling bad for past behavior as an excuse to put off feeling good about yourself.
- **Self-forgiveness, responsibility** — forgiving yourself for past behavior and being responsible in the future.

- *Taking things for granted* — not appreciating things around you, especially things that you had to work for (like sobriety).
- **Gratitude** — thankfulness for what you have, for your life.

Step Five:

> Admitted to God, to ourselves, and to another human being the exact nature of our wrongs.

If we were honest and thorough with our personal inventory (Step Four), we have identified many of our character defects and have a record of the harm we caused others. We can see exactly where our behavior has been insane and how our life has been unmanageable.

In Step Five, it is important to admit your wrongs to yourself, to your Higher Power, and then to talk them over with another person. This could be a minister, counselor, or your sponsor. What's important is that it's somebody who you trust won't judge you or reveal what you say to anyone else.

Carmen:

"I had a lot of guilt about my past. I did a lot of lousy things, and I had a hard time facing up to it all.

"Once I did Step Five, I felt like a ton was lifted from my shoulders. I talked over my personal inventory with my minister and I really feel like I have put my past behind me, like I've forgiven myself, and I can go forward with a clean slate."

. . . talk over these wrongs with one other person.

Step Six:

Were entirely ready to have God remove all these defects of character.

and

Step Seven:

Humbly asked Him to remove our shortcomings.

Step Six and Seven are simply saying that we need to make a commitment to live our life by our positive traits and avoid hurting ourselves and others. Again, we are not going to be perfect, we're human.

Wayne:

"Steps Six and Seven are ongoing for me. I can say in my mind, *Of course I don't want any defects. Of course I'm ready to have my defects removed,* but in my heart, it's a different story. I use my defects to my advantage, you know, like if I'm in a pity bag. I get attention from that. It's really unhealthy, but I know that's why I do it. So I need to get to a point where I can say, 'Yes, I am ready to give up this negative behavior' and then let go of it and say, 'Lord, help me out and help me to be more aware of how I affect others.'

"That doesn't mean that I'm never going to fall back into negative behavior. It's an ongoing process. I need to accept myself, but I need to strive for change too."

Step Eight:

Made a list of all persons we had harmed, and became willing to make amends to them all.

Step Nine:

Made direct amends to such people wherever possible, except when to do so would injure them or others.

Steps Eight and Nine also work together. These two Steps are saying that in order to stay sober, we have to be willing to look back and see how our drinking and other drug use has affected those around us. If we regret the things we've done, we need to be willing to take responsibility for and correct the wrongs we've done to others — when possible.

Paulo:

"Oh man, I was straight for almost a year before I even realized that there *were* Steps Eight and Nine! Once I finally figured out that it might be a good idea for me to make some amends, it really seemed overwhelming.

"The first thing I did was start to look at the different groups of people that I had hung around with. You know, I had hung around with all kinds of people, switched friends a lot and that kind of thing.

. . . we need to be willing to correct the wrongs we've done to others.

Then, I had to think about the different places that I had worked, different schools I had gone to, relatives I had stolen from, girls I used — the list goes on and on. I figured there's no way I can make amends to everybody! I was looking at it like it was just one big hassle.

"Once I started to talk to people and acknowledge what I had done to them and say that I was sorry or whatever, I realized that it wasn't a hassle at all. It was great! Most of them said, 'No problem," or that I shouldn't feel bad, but mostly I think it really touched them. Some of them couldn't believe it — especially the ones that I stole money from and paid back.

"I think Steps Eight and Nine are important because if you have things from your past you feel bad or guilty about, it's very easy to use those kinds of bad feelings as an excuse to go back to using.

"The easiest way to handle Steps Eight and Nine is to, first, just talk to people that you feel suffered the most from your using and then talk to others as you see them or as it comes up. But don't make it seem so much like work. I mean, I know there are some people I'll never be able to pay back, but I'm trying. Don't forget that *you* need to forgive yourself too.

"Most people will tell you that you can't control the outcome, you know, how people will react, but that you're only responsible for the effort."

Step Ten:

Continued to take personal inventory and when we were wrong promptly admitted it.

This means continuing to be aware of our character defects and assets, and if we're having problems or thinking negatively, to be honest about it. It's important not to use this Step for self-punishment but as a chance each day to change and grow in the program.

Amelia:

"Most people look at Step Ten and say, 'Yeah, yeah, I already do that,' but I don't know how many people really do. I mean, it's hard sometimes not to be defensive or to be really honest with yourself about character defects. I know sometimes when I realize that I'm people-pleasing, I have to force myself to change my behavior. It's just such a habit for me. I need to stop what I'm doing and say, 'It's okay if I don't have a smile on my face all the time. It's okay if I feel like being a bitch.' Usually I don't even notice that I'm falling into old behavior until much later, but then I deal with it."

The Big Book recommends doing Step Ten at the end of each day as a way to let go of that day's problems and start the next day with a clean slate.

Step Eleven:

Sought through prayer and meditation to improve our conscious contact with God *as we understood Him*, praying only for knowledge of His will for us and the power to carry that out.

Step Eleven can seem very complex. Everyone has a different way of defining prayer and meditation and looking for spiritual guidance. Here's a simple definition: *Prayer* is when we talk to our Higher Power. *Meditation* is when we listen. Step Eleven is about staying spiritually aware in our lives, One Day at a Time.

Michael:

"For me, Steps Ten and Eleven work together; meditation is going over my day in my mind just before I go to sleep at night. I look back on the day and give myself positive strokes, and I also look at

what I could've handled better. I always am
thankful that I've stayed sober another day."

Patrick:

"Working Step Eleven also kind of works with Step
Three. I mean, I just kind of 'let things happen'; I
look inside myself for 'signs' for what to do, and I
try to trust my intuition more. That may sound off
the wall, but it works for me."

Maria:

"Step Eleven for me means to live spiritually,
which means just doing the right thing. If I'm
confronted with choices that are hard, I ask myself, 'What's the *right* thing to do?' If you follow the
truth and follow what's in your heart, you can't go
wrong."

*. . . praying only for
knowledge of His will . . .*

Jody:

"If you pray and stuff like that, you'll feel closer to God. Feeling closer to your Higher Power, feeling good about yourself, and feeling good toward others will show through in your actions."

Jordon:

"I try to look for guidance by looking to others in need. People in need of help are just everywhere! I think God is guiding each of us to help each other by the fact that there are always people around us who need help."

Sara:

"I do try to meditate every day. It's important for me to have some quiet time for myself.

"I think Step Eleven is talking about living each day with more love in our heart and our life. I think a lot of young people just see this as unreachable . . . it just seems hard to imagine walking around every day with a smile on our face and love in our heart . . . it seems kind of mindless, you know.

"How Step Eleven works for me, though, is to just be accepting of myself and realistic in my goals. If I can be more accepting of those around me, then I have improved my conscious contact with God, because I think that we all are a part of God."

Curt:

"Step Eleven means having faith and trust."

Step Twelve:

Having had a spiritual awakening as the result of these steps, we tried to carry this message to alcoholics [or "addicts"], and to practice these principles in all our affairs.

When you work all of the Steps, you'll probably find you are more in harmony with others — and your life will have more meaning. Because of this, you may want to let others know that they can live clean and sober too.

Leilin:

(An eighteen-year-old alcoholic who wants to become a doctor.)

"When I first got sober, I thought, *This is great! My whole life is changed!* And I wanted the whole world to experience what I had. I had a ton of old drinking friends who could definitely stand to go straight, and I was ready to change the world.

"Everybody in AA who had been there awhile discouraged me from trying to save the world. They tried to explain to me that people are turned off by preaching and that there's a lot of denial out there. I just kept thinking that being sober and going straight would be good for everyone, and how are they going to find out about it unless I convince them, and what if their lives just get worse and worse?

"Well, it's a good thing I finally got the message through my thick skull or I could've really turned off a bunch of people. People don't want to be put down and told that what they're doing is wrong. They will automatically put their defenses up.

"What I learned to do is just be a good example. I know that sounds too easy to do, but it works. I almost make it a rule to never talk to anyone about their drinking or drug use. I just talk about *my* use. It makes life a hell of a lot easier. If I've got to take responsibility for everyone else going straight, then it's my responsibility if they use too, right? I can't deal with that."

. . . I was ready to change the world.

That's Too Much to Remember

You may be thinking, *You've got to be kidding! How do you expect me to stay straight if I've got to remember all that!*

Please don't think that you have to remember and follow these Steps, word for word, all the time. They are guidelines, suggestions, and no one has ever followed them perfectly. It is not important to start worrying about how or when you'll accomplish each Step. The important thing is to go to meetings and take the information you need and use it, and leave the rest until you are ready for it.

Your First Meeting

AA and NA are in the phone book. You can call and find out where and when meetings are, usually through a central "intergroup" number. Some meetings are closed, meaning only people recovering from alcoholism are invited. Others are open so that nonrecovering friends or people who are interested can attend.

There are various approaches and formats for meetings. Some common ones are:

- *Speaker's meeting.* Someone in the program will talk on a topic related to recovery or tell his or her history of alcohol use and how the person came to the program.
- *Topic meeting.* A topic is selected for the meeting, such as procrastination, acceptance, patience, or fellowship, and members discuss how the topic affects them. If you don't have anything to say, you can pass.
- *Step/Tradition meeting.* One Step or Tradition is selected and discussed. The Steps may be covered in order from week to week, beginning again with Step One after Step Twelve.

- *Big Book meeting.* One chapter is read aloud from *Alcoholics Anonymous* — the Big Book — and discussed.
- *Call up meeting.* Everyone gets a number when they enter the meeting and whoever's number is drawn tells his or her story to the group.
- *New member's meeting.* New members are always welcome at any meeting; however, some chapters do have specific weekly meetings designed for new people.

There are other Twelve Step groups for people who aren't alcoholic, but who struggle with the problems of living with an alcoholic or other addict. Some of them are Al-Anon (for people in a relationship with a chemically dependent person); Alateen (for children still living at home whose parents are chemically dependent); and Adult Children of Alcoholics (for adults who were raised by an alcoholic parent).

People whose main problem is with drugs other than alcohol can attend meetings of Narcotics Anonymous. And significant others of NA members can attend Nar-Anon.

Not all communities will offer all of the different types of meetings listed here, but most offer a variety of meetings. For their first meeting, many young people find it's easier to attend a young people's or a new members' meeting.

The Time Has Come
To Take the Plunge

Going to your first AA or NA meeting can be terrifying, so here are a few tips to help you out:

- If you know anyone who goes to AA or NA, ask him or her to take you to a meeting.
- If you go to your first meeting alone, try to go a few minutes early. Introduce yourself to the first person you see, and explain to that person that this is your

first meeting and you'd appreciate it if he or she could show you the ropes. I know that it's terrifying to do this, but most of the time you'll receive a warm welcome, and if you don't, talk to the next person you see.

- Pick up any free literature that's available. The more you learn about the program, the better. You won't feel so out-of-it and you'll get more help in meeting your own needs.

- When the meeting starts, people introduce themselves by saying "Hi, I'm _____, and I'm an alcoholic." When it's your turn to introduce yourself, if you're not sure you're alcoholic, you can just say something like "Hi, I'm _____, and this is my first meeting" or "Hi, I'm _____, and I'm here to see what AA is like." No one will find this strange at all. You may even meet other new people at the meeting.

- When the conversation moves around the room during the meeting and it's your turn to talk, you can either say something or pass. If you feel comfortable enough, it's really helpful to talk about why you want to be at the meeting. You'll probably be amazed at how supportive everyone can be. And the sooner you say something, the sooner you'll feel a part of the group. In some meetings, other members respond or give feedback, but in most, people just listen with a silent acceptance of whatever anyone has to say, as long as it isn't disruptive to others' desire to stay straight.

- After the meeting, you can ask the person who ran the

Going to your first AA meeting can be terrifying . . .

meeting, or someone else, if there is a phone list available of people willing to take calls if you should feel in danger of using or just need support. Not all chapters will have a phone list, but calling can be an important part of staying straight — phoning instead of using.

- Try to stay after the meeting and introduce yourself to as many people as possible. I know this can be awkward, but usually you'll find many are very open and friendly. Often there's an opportunity to go out after the meeting and socialize.

- If you didn't enjoy your first meeting, DON'T GIVE UP! Try meetings at different days and times. Most likely, you *will* find a meeting that you feel comfortable with.

. . . phoning instead of drinking.

Go to a Meeting
And See What You Think

Justin:

> *(A sixteen-year-old with long blond hair who went straight without going through treatment. He just started going to AA.)*

"I started getting high when I was nine years old. I used to hang around with a guy who was a lot older than me and, because I was just curious about getting high, I started smoking pot with him. I didn't start drinking until about a year later.

"I was kind of shy and most of the time I would get drunk or high with only one or two other people. I didn't go to parties until I got older.

"I really didn't communicate with my parents during this time. I don't think they knew what I was doing, although I think my older sisters knew.

"Life was really boring to me. That's why I drank. There just didn't seem like anything better to do.

"About two years ago, when I was fourteen, I went out to visit my uncle in Vermont. We had a six-hour drive back to his house. While we were in the car, he asked me a bunch of questions about my use. My uncle is like 'Joe Alcoholic,' you know. He's been straight and going to AA for a long time. He said if I wanted, I could go to an AA meeting with him.

"I went to a meeting and I really liked it. It was better than the drinking and drugs, because it didn't wear off. I kept going to meetings for the whole month I was in Vermont.

"When I came back home, I really didn't want to admit to my folks that I was going to meetings, so I stopped going. I started drinking again.

"After I had been drinking and using for a while, I talked to my uncle on the phone and he said, 'Look, just go to a meeting there and see what you think.' Once I started going to meetings at home, I went straight again, right away.

"There are a lot of people who say, 'My worst day straight is better than my best day drinking.' Well, for me, that's a bunch of shit. I've had some really bad days straight too. I just like myself better when I'm straight.

"I don't think about the future. I know I don't want to drink today, but I don't want to think I can't have anything for the rest of my life.

"You know, just because you go straight doesn't mean you have to become a saint or something. You can still get crazy, you know. Only now, you can let go and have a good time without hurting yourself or anybody else."

What About Sponsors?

A sponsor is someone who has been with the AA or NA program for quite a while and has some solid straight time. A sponsor agrees to help you on your path of sobriety, especially in the beginning. Your sponsor can go with you to meetings, tell you about his or her own struggle when first going straight, and be there when you need support. Most people like to touch base with their sponsor about once a week.

If you have gone through a treatment program, people there may give you a list of possible sponsors. Many times, the potential sponsors are people who have gone through the same treatment program.

Also, most AA or NA chapters have a list of people who are willing to sponsor others.

Contrary to what some might think, someone you've known for a long time *does not* necessarily make a good sponsor. You may be better off starting a brand new relationship than to expect a friend to have the kind of impartial commitment that a sponsor needs. It's also best that your sponsor is at least a little older than you and not a prospect for a romantic relationship. Sexual complications can really muddy up this kind of relationship and jeopardize the most important thing it's there for — mutual sobriety.

Most people in AA agree that a sponsor makes the path of sobriety easier, less stressful, and even more fun. A sponsor is there for you when you need someone to listen and offer his or her experience. A sponsor's responsibilities *do not* include preaching, telling you how to live your life, or invading your space. Somebody becomes a sponsor for his or her *own* sobriety — to work the Twelfth Step. Not to take care of people or act as recovery experts.

Many times, if someone is negative on the idea of having a sponsor, it's because they had a bad experience with one. Sponsors are human and they are working on their character defects just as we all are. As with anything, there are good sponsors and there are ones that are not so good. So keep this in mind when looking for a sponsor and realize that you are not obligated to stay with a sponsor you don't feel comfortable with.

Probably one of the most important relationships you will build in AA is with your sponsor, so it's very important to find a different one if you don't feel you're getting what you need. In fact, many people suggest having two or three regular sponsors. Most likely there will be someone out there for you, but it may not be the first person you try.

Having a sponsor has many advantages.

- It's nice to have one person who really knows you and your situation.
- It helps your other sober relationships because you're not depending on your friends to meet all of your needs.
- It's nice to have someone who'll be honest and objective and who you can call nearly anytime you need to without feeling that you're imposing.

"She Is Always There When I Need Her"

Pauline:

"I got my first sponsor right out of treatment. She was recommended to me by a friend who'd also just gotten out. She was her sponsor and she figured that I would like her too. Well, I did like her, but I still decided to find a different sponsor, because we just didn't make the kind of connection that I thought we should.

"My second sponsor worked out great, at first. She was really into the program and was concerned about me and how I was doing. Things seemed to be going good for a few months. I'm not sure when thing started going downhill, but they did. The relationship just kind of turned negative. She was always taking my inventory and trying to tell me what to do — who to hang around with and everything. I'm sure she meant well, but it was just a drag. So then, I thought I might be better off without a sponsor for a while.

"I didn't feel deprived or bad at all when I didn't have a sponsor. I felt like I had a good support system, and things went really well. The main reason I decided to find a sponsor again is that sometimes when I needed to talk, I just felt guilty dumping on my friends and family all the time.

"I was at a Big Book meeting and I was listening to this woman who I thought was really cool. She seemed to have a good handle on who she was. One night, I ended up having coffee with her. We really hit it off, so I asked her to be my sponsor.

"Ever since that night, I've been a big advocate of sponsors. Gerri and I have the best relationship. She is always there when I need her and, most of the time, she has the perfect thing to say. I don't think it's totally one-sided either. I mean, I think she gets a lot out of our relationship too.

"Anyway, I think that sponsors are great. It's just a matter of finding the right one . . . or two."

If I Don't Go to AA Am I Going to Go Back to Using?

There are no guarantees with AA or NA. It is not guaranteed that, if you go, you'll stay straight and if you don't go, you'll relapse. There are recovering people who don't go to AA or NA and still have rewarding, growing lives, and, of course, there are those who don't. You need to know what will be good for *you*. Going to AA or NA and working the Twelve Step program is a choice.

A place to meet friends . . .

To sum up, here are some of the things that AA or NA can give you:

- An opportunity to meet people who are in the same situation as you, so you don't feel like the "only one."
- A place to have fun without the self-destructive behavior that goes with drinking.
- Guidance and a support system for personal growth and recovery. A place to share your feelings and a place where you'll be accepted for who you are.

Shawn:

"Thinking about going to AA? Do it! You've got nothing to lose and everything to gain."

Now I Know Everything There Is to Know About AA, Right?

Afraid not, but enough to get you started. AA is going to mean something different to each person who attends.

Some people look at AA and say, "I don't get it. It's a bunch of contradictions. First you say I need to get my life under control and then you say I need to give up control and be powerless. On one hand, I should accept my character defects and, on the other hand, I should be working for their removal. So what's the deal?"

AA deals with all of these. I think one of the reasons why AA has worked for so many, for so many years, is because it deals with a range of different principles for personal growth, while leaving each person free to choose how to apply them. It promotes a life of balance.

It has been said time and time again it's impossible for anyone to follow the AA program perfectly, just as it's impossible to have perfect balance or perfect awareness or perfect honesty. But if you go to AA or to another Twelve Step group, you'll find a framework you can work with that has helped more alcoholics stay sober than anything else going.

AA promotes balance in life.

Spirituality,
Or
Here They Go with That
God Stuff Again!

Climbing the Stairway to Heaven

My first week in treatment, I heard stories from the other inmates (that's what I called them then — inmates) about a guy named Randy who had just left the center and was sent to a facility for the mentally ill. Rumors flew:

- "He flipped out on some bad acid."
- "Yeah, he thinks his best friend is Satan."
- "He's in bad shape, man. I think he's still trippin'."

Truth was, Randy was still tripping. He did some peyote buttons and had a nightmarish evening before ending up in a hospital emergency room and then treatment.

He did think his best friend was Satan, and when he walked into the treatment center and saw the Twelve Steps on a plaque on the wall, he thought he had found his salvation. He latched onto the program immediately. He thought he was climbing the stairway to heaven with each Step. Anything a counselor told him to do, he did with intensity. If he was told to do twenty-five sit-ups, he did them like they were his last act, with perfect movements. He was striving for complete harmony.

One day he was found wandering down the hall, naked. He told the counselors that he didn't see the problem since we are all children of God.

He stayed high from that one bad trip almost continuously for the six weeks he was in chemical dependency treatment, and he was still tripping through most of his six weeks on the mental health unit, where he was diagnosed as psychotic and schizophrenic.

While I was struggling with Steps Two and Three and having a hard time applying any spirituality in my life, I would think about Randy. I thought, *It's no wonder I'm having such a tough time with this stuff. You have to be whacked out of your mind to get it.* I felt like I was never going to have the same kind of commitment that Randy had, so what was the point.

The good news is that Randy eventually snapped out of it and was released. He has been straight for about eight years now and has a wonderful life with his wife and two kids. Oh, he's still trying to live spiritually, but it's in a totally different way — a more relaxed way.

Sometimes I think Randy's turnabout was healthier for me than it was for him. It felt so good to know

What was your spirituality like when you were using?

that no one could be perfectly spiritual. Knowing this meant I could quit bouncing off the walls, kick back, and take time to develop a relationship with my Higher Power.

The purpose of this chapter is not to talk you into believing in a God or convince you that you'll be unfulfilled unless you become superspiritual. Mainly you'll hear stories from those who've been there — chemically dependent young people who are now straight and finding their own ways to work a spiritual program.

What Was Your Spirituality Like When You Were Using?

As we grew up, each of us was introduced to a different idea of spirituality. A lot of us got most of our religious training from our parents. Some of us had in-depth discussions with friends, or maybe we read about other religions or got into the supernatural or paranormal as a way to develop our own spiritual ideas.

While we were using, most of us prayed (or more like bargained) when we were in trouble. You know, "If you get me out of this, God, I swear I'll never . . ."

The one thing we all have in common is that we had a higher power while we were using — drugs. Alcohol and other drugs told us who we were going to hang out with, how we would spend our time, when we would attend school or work, how we would spend our money, what our image would be, and controlled practically every other aspect of our life. We became very good at turning our life and our will over to alcohol and other drugs.

Marty:

"My parents were divorced when I was twelve. It was right about then that I started getting high and drinking and stuff.

"Anyway, my sister and I lived with my mom and as a family we always went to church and Bible studies and stuff, but it was really only 'cause my mom wanted us to go. My dad wasn't religious at all.

"After the divorce, my dad hardly ever came to see us or anything, so I took it real personal, you know, like he didn't like me or something. I wanted him to like me. I wanted to get along with him.

"When I did see him, he would bitch about the church and call it all a bunch of crap, so I would agree with him and we would bitch about it together. It was a way for me to get along with him. It was like we had something in common. You know, I just wanted him to *like* me.

"As I got heavier into using, I hung onto those beliefs and a lot of my friends thought the same thing, you know, that the only people who go to church are a bunch of hypocrites.

"Now, I'm not trying to please anyone but myself. I mean I consider myself really spiritual, but it's my own beliefs — not really my mom's or my dad's."

Tammy:

"Well, when I was little, I think my stuffed animals were my Higher Power. Seriously . . . I didn't really know anything about God. We went to church on Sunday, but the only reason I liked Sunday was because we got to go out for pizza, you know, that was about it.

"I never have paid any attention to the God part of it. When I was using it was like 'God get me out of this,' you know, 'I'll go to church until I'm eighteen' . . . but, I never, not even when I cleaned up, I never really paid attention to the God thing because Christianity's God, the Bible's God is not mine. I don't agree with a lot of the things that were in that . . . I just accept Higher Power instead of God."

Chad:

"I used to believe in Jah, the Rastafarian God. I used to claim that as my religion a lot and now it's like I believe in all their concepts and stuff, except for smoking pot. I don't do that anymore, so that kind of makes it difficult for me."

SERVICES
10:00
11:00
12:00
"NEARER THY GOD.."

Michelle:

"In sixth grade I quit believing in God because my mom would drag me to church and I got sick and tired of it, so I just told her that I didn't believe in it. After awhile I believed that I didn't believe in it. I'm just learning how to believe in a God.

"Before I got in treatment, I talked to this guy . . . I have to laugh about it now. He had been through treatment quite a few times and he was still drinking. We were talking about Higher Power stuff and he says 'you have to have a Higher Power' and I'd say 'I'm my Higher Power. I'm God.' You know, I have to laugh now, because I was thinkin' I was God. I thought, *What are you talking about this God bullshit?*"

Matt:

"I went along with everything in my family, but none of it ever really meant anything to me. Even my bar mitzvah . . . it was no big deal. I just did whatever my parents thought I should do."

Janet:

"My spirituality when I was using was nothing, just nothing. I never even thought about it . . . I don't know, even if it came up in conversation, I had no interest in talking or thinking about it — no more interest than I would have if something like needlepoint came up — basically none."

Tyler:

"Oh, I prayed all the time when I was using, but it was always only when I was in trouble or something — which was all the time.

"You know, 'Oh God, please get me out of this.' It's easy to find religion real quick when you're spread-eagled on the hood of a cop car."

Sierra:

"I used to say my prayers at night when I was little, still do. Like when I was in treatment I'd be laying in bed, you know, and I wouldn't put my hands together or nothin'. I'd just say them when I was layin' there, you know, to myself and either ask or thank Him for something. Just for like how the day went . . . I guess I never realized before that there were things to be thankful for."

Karen:

"I did believe in God, but I think it was based on fear. It was kind of like 'What if I didn't believe in God and something horrible happened?' I knew there was some Power in control, because mom and dad had been through treatment and told me about that type of spirituality. When I started using, I believed in something, but I just didn't want to let a Higher Power have any power in my life.

"When I got so down that I tried suicide, that's when I said, 'God, I know what my choices are. I have to get straight or I'll die' and I kind of turned it over to my Higher Power. In my head that's what I was doing."

So Now I'm Supposed To Go to Church Every Week?

Religion and spirituality are not the same thing. Religion is something organized by a *group* of people, and there is usually a group philosophy or way of thinking that the people who belong to that particular religion agree with.

Spirituality is a *personal* philosophy or way of thinking. It's made up of your individual experience or contact with a Higher Power. Your spirituality changes as you change. Religion is a fairly fixed set of ideas.

You can decide for yourself whether or not you want to be part of an organized religion or go to church or temple. Just remember, you're not any less spiritual if you don't belong to an organized religion.

Some people like to belong to a church to set aside some time to spend with their Higher Power each week or to meet people whose beliefs are similar to theirs. If you decide you want to do this, check around, read about different religions, and attend different churches until you find one you're comfortable with.

What Did You Think When You First Read About God and a Higher Power in the Twelve Steps?

Jon:

"My mom is an atheist and I never had religion. In treatment I really questioned it, you know, and I had a hell of a time with Steps Two and Three. I had to write my answers to a bunch of questions about my beliefs in a workbook and it's like 'How do I answer these?' I don't know. . . . I believe in God now."

April:

"Steps Two and Three were no big deal. I mean they specifically say 'God, *as we understood Him.*' That could mean anything. I just had to figure out what a Higher Power was to *me.*"

Michelle:

"I thought this Higher Power idea isn't logical and I'm a logical person. I like things in logical order — logical reasons why it would be there. I'm trying to get myself out of that logical mind-set."

Todd:

"By the time I got to treatment, I was ready for a program like the Steps.

"Coke took everything from me, you know, it destroyed every aspect of my life. I was a real mess — physically, mentally, emotionally — and when I saw Steps Two and Three it was like 'Wow, this is it. This is what I need.' I was totally ready."

Sandy:

"I thought 'Oh great, a bunch of Jesus freaks. Just what I need. They probably walk around going *Jesus loves you.*' I thought it would be a total turnoff. Of course, I found out I was totally wrong."

Karen:

"I knew it was important, but I hadn't given it any thought. I just wasn't in the mood to think about my Higher Power or anything like that. I was still at the point where I was grateful to be alive . . . because that was the choice I gave my Higher Power. I said when I hit bottom, 'Either you kill me or I'll wake up in the morning and I'll have to sober up and change my life.' In that way, my Higher Power made the choice for me."

What Made You Come To Believe in a Higher Power?

I think it's interesting how Step Two is worded:

Came to believe that a Power greater than ourselves could restore us to sanity.

To me, the statement "Came to believe . . ." means that believing happens over time. How much time? Who

. . . it was hard for me to take time for this process. I want everything NOW.

96

knows. Maybe coming to believe in a Higher Power is an ever-changing, ever-evolving process. Since I am a member of the "instant gratification" generation, it was hard for me to take the time for this process. I want everything NOW.

"Came to believe" just means realizing the *slightest possibility* that there could be a Power greater than ourselves. It was easy for drugs to become greater than us, but now it's time to find a better way.

Janine:

"Once I started listening to the other people in group, listening to their struggle, it got easier for me. Every one of them had a different idea of a Higher Power. I agreed with some and not with others.

"Also, the more I talked with people who'd been straight awhile, the more I realized they had something I didn't — some kind of confidence or something. I don't know what it was, I just wanted it too."

Jon:

"I figured out that religion is *man-made* and spirituality is just God, you know."

Michelle:

"When I first went straight, I was going through a bunch of shit with my boyfriend and my best friend. I was having a hard time. I went for a walk one night — I was crying — up this hill we have by our house and I just kind of fell down because I wanted the pain to go away. I looked up at the sky and said 'Hey, you want to take the pain away? Take the pain away. I don't want it anymore.' And it went away and I went home smiling . . . I went home thinking 'I found something. I grew. I grew a little bit.' I felt like it was okay. That's when I first started thinking I need to try to believe in something *out there* because I can't totally depend on myself and I need something else besides a human to be dependent on."

Tyler:

"People just kept saying to me 'You've been doing it your way for a long time and look where it's gotten you.' They were right. I didn't want to admit it, and it took me a long time to do that, but they were right and I finally just had to find a way to make the Steps work for me instead of fighting them all the time."

What Is Your Higher Power?

This is a question many of us struggle with. Sometimes it's a good idea to start with what we've been taught in the past — our religious training and other ideas about spirituality — and see if there are any parts that we still accept.

Whatever we call this Power greater than ourselves, many of us need to experience it both as a part of us working within, and yet outside of ourselves too, working in the world or universe. We haven't had good luck with running solely on our own impulses. We need to feel a positive force in the world around us that we can turn to for guidance. Yet if our Higher Power is totally "out there," it's hard to feel connected to it and take responsibility for our spirituality.

This reminds me of the joke about the guy who is in a flood and the water is rising around him, so he climbs to the roof of his house. A woman rows up in a boat and says, "Get in. I'll bring you to safety." He says, "No thanks. God will save me from drowning."

The water rises so high that he is standing on the chimney to stay above it. A helicopter hovers above him and someone calls down for him to climb aboard. He says, "No thanks. I have faith. God will save me."

The man drowns and when he meets God at heaven's gate, he says, "God, why didn't you save me?" and God says, "I sent you a boat and a helicopter."

Sometimes we make our Higher Power too mysterious or too far out. We're easier on ourselves if we keep it simple — something we can imagine as possible and really believe in.

Coming to know your Higher Power is very personal and often difficult. Take your time. Be willing to challenge and change your ideas. You'll know it inside when you're comfortable with it.

Keep in mind, having a Higher Power is not so much a system of belief as it is a way of life.

Michelle:

"Now, I'm just learning. I have a hard time. I try to believe in God — I call it God because Higher Power is too long — and I figure, looking at God in my way, that there is a being up there, but it's not human, it's not anything, just kind of a blob. Just something I can believe in."

Matt:

"I think the Steps should read 'God, *as we understood* It,' not '*Him*,' because most of the people I know think of their Higher Power as a force instead of a Him or a person.

"For me, my Higher Power is kind of like a collection of souls. I mean, each one of us has a soul and each one of us is a little piece of God and all of us together complete the Power. This includes all souls, even people who've died. Their souls live on."

Tammy:

"I've been thinking a lot about it lately. I got a book from the library called *The Skeptical Feminist* by Barbara Walker and it's really good because she writes a lot about the different things that are in the Bible and how they're contradictory, how they're hypocritical, how they're just so confused, you know. Then she'd start writing about the 'Goddess,' which is a religion and belief that was around, you know, ever since the beginning of time. I don't like putting a title on it, you know, I just identify with the Goddess better because it's female. I don't relate to the unforgiving, harsh, cruel, vindictive male that a lot of people have made God out to be. I don't criticize religion because men wrote the Bible and men interpreted the Bible. I just don't to deal with it. It doesn't include me.

"I mean a lot of women coming into the program are not interested in 'God,' because 'God' has let men treat women bad. I didn't really know about the Goddess until probably about a year and a half ago, but I never really paid much attention because I was too busy trying to get myself settled into the program. . . . I don't think you can really concentrate on different subjects like this until you're more stable, you know, 'cause if you immediately jump in and try to find a whole different religion, you're going to screw yourself up, 'cause you're so unsure of yourself."

Chad:

"Even before I started using I didn't believe in God. I believe in evolution. I think it's pretty possible that there was a big boom way, way back. . . . I think that mankind could have formed from the apes.

"Being in nature, just being out in everything, I can feel something there. If someone is around me and is talking about using, I can't be with my Higher Power then. If I can just be out in nature by myself, I can feel it.

"Any two people together or anybody with a day more sobriety than me is more powerful than I am, so if I can just talk to someone who's in recovery or just go to a meeting, that's my Higher Power."

Jon:

"I don't think God is an old man or an old woman. It's just a Power — like love."

Karen:

"I can't always picture what my Higher Power is, but I can picture what It does. It gives me good feelings and shows me that there's something else that's in control."

Joe:

"One of the staff people in treatment said, 'Believe in the God you see with your own eyes.' He said that his Higher Power is like a God he sees with his own eyes, you know, not the God that everybody goes to church for.

"At first my Higher Power was my AA and NA group and it still is sort of. I'm still working on another Higher Power and that Higher Power is like something I see with my own eyes, you know, he's got long hair like Jesus did. I'm not saying He is Jesus, only that He's got long hair. I don't know, that's just the way I see Him — long hair, cool, a laid-back kind of guy without a care in the world. He's just there. He's really with it."

Brandon:

"After I was straight for about a year, I decided that I wanted to study more about spirituality. I always followed the Steps, but I was just interested in other viewpoints.

"I studied everything — Buddhism, Hinduism, Bahaism, Christianity. What was neat was that I got something out of each one. For instance, I thought it was neat how in Eastern religions they think of God as being within us not 'out there' and that you *listen* to God, not *pray* to it.

"I think after reading so much, the religion I agree with most is the one that the Native Americans follow. They have respect for *all* life and for the earth and stuff. It's really cool."

What Role Does Spirituality Play in Your Recovery

Step Three:

> Made a decision to turn our will and our lives
> over to the care of God *as we understood Him.*

I couldn't believe it when I first discovered that Step
Three started with the words, "Made a decision. . . ."
Somehow I missed that part for a long time. It doesn't
read, "We turned our lives over. . . ." It says, "Made a
decision to turn our will and our lives over. . . ." What a
discovery!

I can make a decision to get my hair cut, but that
doesn't mean I have actually done it. I can make a decision to go back to school and yet not sign up for a single
class. To make a decision to turn my will and life over to
the care of God simply means to *want* to try a different
way than I have in the past. It means I *want* to make
different choices for myself.

Maybe I don't always let go of all parts of myself —
like my anger — but I can still decide not to get high and
decide to *want* to turn it over or get rid of it or deal with it.

April:

> "I guess being spiritual makes me feel more like
> I'm an important part of the world. You know, if
> there is a Higher Power and It did create all of this,
> then I must be here for some reason, you know,
> some kind of purpose. It helps keep me straight —
> in more ways than one."

Joey:

> "Well, spirituality just helps me to be more laid-
> back. When I was using, I was constantly getting
> pissed off over every little thing. Now, I don't let
> too much bother me and I mean I *really* don't. I
> figure things are meant to be."

Michelle:

> "I can't rely on myself all the time. I need someone to hold my hand who I know I can count on and who isn't going to shit out on me. I mean, I can count on my friend, Jon, but he might not always be there. I can't be dependent on him, 'cause it's not fair to him and it's not fair to myself. So I need to lean on something, to believe in something so I *can* feel safe without being dependent on a human, you know. Logically, I have a hard time with it, but I'm learning."

Jon:

> "It's to never be alone. Spirituality keeps my attitude in check."

Anita:

> "I think my Higher Power works through people. Like the people at meetings or just people I trust in my daily life. I listen to their stories and I think about myself, you know, to see if we're the same at all.

> "I don't want to make it sound like I automatically think everything I hear are 'words from God.' It's more like just being on the lookout for ideas that will help me."

Christopher:

> "I just can't even imagine being straight without it. It's just so important. You've just got to be able to lean on something — to turn it over. It doesn't matter if you call it a Higher Power, your higher conscience, or the group, or God, or Fred — you sometimes just need to have an outside release."

Tammy:

"I think it has a kind of a calming effect. I'm more comfortable with it. Before, when I was using, I was angry and violent a lot, usually to protect myself, you know. Now, I realize I don't have to protect myself like that . . . so it's had a real calming effect. I can be tolerant, I can be patient, and I can be gentle, but that doesn't mean I'm the type of woman who wouldn't protest if her son was being murdered or something."

How Do You Work Spirituality Into Your Everyday Life?

Earlier, I mentioned that spirituality is more than a set of beliefs; it's a lifestyle. So what does this mean?

I think the difference is this: if you operate your life on a set of beliefs without spirituality, you might say, "I don't steal because _____ (a book, a person, an institution) says I shouldn't." If you link your beliefs to your spirituality, you might say, "I don't steal because I don't want that type of behavior to be a part of my life."

See the difference? With spirituality, you make choices for yourself based on your values, a new way you've decided to lead your life — a drug-free way.

Chad:

"I have a lot of trouble turning it over because I want things to work out my way and I want to plan it out so it works.

"Writing letters helps you to turn it over, you know. I wrote a resentments letter to my stepdad and now my resentments toward him don't bug me. Just write it down and burn it or throw it away."

Julaine:

"I meditate and read and write. Keeping a journal has been really great too. It's weird, but I think another thing I get from spirituality is energy. It's kind of like feeling like I can do anything."

Jack:

"I don't know. That's a hard question. I don't know if I really do apply it every day. It's no big deal really. It's just kind of there if I need it."

Karen:

"I'm really bad at turning things over. I'm so bad at that. Just lately, with some problems with my dad, I've been getting better at just accepting it and not feeling hopeless. I think part of my not feeling hopeless is from my Higher Power.

"Sometimes I just think about a Higher Power taking care of me and taking care of us. . . . That's how the Higher Power helps me. I just fill myself

. . . writing letters helps you turn it over.

with a little bit of power, you know, the power to get through this. The power to not let all of it affect me, and it works.

"Another thing I do is when I read the Steps, I'll keep putting in 'God' where it says 'Him.' Otherwise it leaves me out, you know. The same with the Big Book. I didn't used to have an opinion because I thought 'Hey, it was written a long time ago, it was the times or whatever. I can live with 'Him' in the Big Book. But now it's like 'they're not talking to me.' I realize that I don't have to like everything about the program to make it work. I can change it so it works for me."

Joe:

"At AA and NA meetings, when people bring up spirituality, I don't really like to talk, but I do anyways. I don't talk long 'cause I don't really like to talk about spirituality. To turn it over, I just sort of walk away from it and take a time-out."

Amelia:

"Since I've gone straight, I've quit smoking, become a vegetarian, started recycling, and made a bunch of other changes in my lifestyle. I think part of the reason I've made changes is because of my spirituality.

"I usually don't tell people because it freaks them out too much. They may think, *I better not follow these Steps or next thing you know I won't be able to eat meat either!* So I try not to talk about it.

"It's just a personal decision. For me, it's happened in stages. I figure if I'm going to be a part of this planet, I need to take care and responsibility for my actions."

Jon:

"For me, Step Three is sort of like letting go. I just sort of say it out loud 'Okay, it's done, there's nothing I can do' or 'This is the way it is. I have to make the best of it.' It's not forgetting about it, just accepting it."

Carmen:

"I'm not really too comfortable talking about my spirituality. You know, some people are like 'God this' and 'My Higher Power that.' I'm just not like that.

"My connection with my Higher Power is personal. Sometimes I'll hear people talking at meetings about some kind of evolved level they've reached with their God and it just seems like a put-down to everyone else, like they're the ones who are *really* spiritual.

"So sometimes I'll talk to someone one-on-one about my spirituality, but I mainly just keep it to myself."

Wayne:

"Turning it over and over and over. I'm serious. Sometimes I have to say, 'I don't want to deal with this. You can have it' forty or fifty times before I really quit thinking about it. Some-times it's only once, but most of the time it's over and over and over."

Toni:

"I don't think of spirituality as praying everyday, like 'Oh God, our Father, Alleluia, Alleluia'. On a day-to-day basis, I try to spend time with animals, with my pets. I spend a lot of time outdoors, go for walks, that kind of thing."

Spirituality Is a Lifelong Journey

It's very common for people to feel that they have a spiritual void or hole inside of them. Everyone has feelings of inadequacy, and events from a person's past may have left an emptiness inside.

When we use chemicals, we are trying to fill up that hole. So when we stop using chemicals, we may not know what to do instead. Sometimes people will try to fill the void with food, relationships, sex, or material things. As you might guess, these solutions are only temporary. As with drugs, the sensation wears off.

Spirituality and learning to love yourself is a step in the right direction. You don't have to buy into everything you hear about spirituality. Just take your time and see what feels good for you. Recovery is not a race! Enjoy yourself. Fill up with the positive and you won't have room for the negative.

Remember the journey is what counts, not only the destination.

In Order to Stay Straight, Do I Have to Be Spiritual?

No. There are many people who stay happily straight without a strictly spiritual program — there are even atheist AA meetings.

Those who've defined their spirituality say it helps, but it is certainly possible to work the Steps your own way, stay straight, and grow without a concept of spirituality.

One way to look at it is this: you don't have to call your new drug-free life spiritual, but it does help to have something outside yourself you can believe in.

Maybe you will have a strong belief in the AA or NA program, or in the people around you who are trying to change the world for the better, or nature, with it's wonderful order, complexity, and balance. You will find something as long as you're willing to grow, change, and explore.

Remember, a Higher Power is something you discover for yourself and that journey of discovery is what spirituality is all about.

Spirituality is hard to get a grip on.

Sexuality, *Or* Some Things You May Not Have Known You Wanted to Know About Sex

Sexuality — A Hot Topic

Okay, admit it. This is the first chapter you turned to, isn't it? I'm sure it's only because you're wondering, "What does sexuality have to do with being straight?" Sure.

Sex and sexuality are topics that most of us would like to know and talk more about. But this isn't easy for some of us because of the way we've been raised or because of the confusing messages society gives us about sex.

Your desire to be sexually involved may be even stronger now that you're not using.

111

Also, our sexuality may have been distorted by our drinking and other drug use. Maybe we wonder, now that we're straight, what part sex will play in our life.

It's likely that your desire to be sexually involved may be even stronger now that you're no longer screwed up by the chemicals you used to put into your body. Some recovering people even make the mistake of turning the high of sexual excitement into a substitute for drugs.

Most people who go straight find out that they have more options for dealing with their sexual feelings and deciding what kind of sexual lifestyle they want to lead.

In this chapter, you'll see how some other recovering young people have handled their sexuality and perhaps you'll come to some decisions about your own sexuality now that you're straight.

April:

> "When I went straight, I thought it would be no problem to deal with my sexuality. I just figured I was not going to go to bed with *anyone* for a long time.

> "Well, little did I know that I would actually find someone that I wanted to become sexually involved with. Then it was like total confusion! Should I or shouldn't I!"

Sex Before Sobering Up

Sometimes, looking back at your sexuality while you were using can help you identify some of the issues you need to examine more, now.

Julaine:

> "When I was using, I slept around a lot. Sometimes I was in a blackout and a lot of the times I hardly knew the guys.

"I have so much shame about it. I feel really scummy . . . and angry. So many guys used me and took advantage of my condition. I'm not so sure I even agreed to it half the time.

"Now I just want to get over these feelings and get on with my life. I just dread the thought of running into any of those guys."

Mark:

"I haven't had sex yet . . . I mean, I've never gone all the way. I've had girlfriends and made out and stuff, but never intercourse.

"I guess when I was using I didn't really have any interest, you know, pot was my girlfriend. I didn't really have any sex drive.

"Part of me wishes that I would have just gotten it over with when I was loaded. It may have been easier 'cause I wouldn't have had any feelings about it. No regrets.

"Honestly, I guess I'm happy, though, that my first time I'll be straight and it will mean something. I'm nervous about it too, but I know I won't have any regrets."

Tammy:

"I don't think I could ever let myself get close to anyone. There was one guy and I feel real bad about what happened between the two of us, because he was really a nice guy, you know. I mean we got along in a lot of ways. I remember when we first started going out he said, 'Well, if you wanted to straighten up, we could probably do it together.' He'd been through treatment and at that point there was no way I was going to stop using. He went out with me anyway, but then I lost him.

"I scared him off, 'cause I didn't understand then that there was more to life than getting loaded and getting laid. I thought that's what I was good for. You know, you give me the drugs and I'll take care of whatever needs you have. That's all I thought there was."

Michael:

"I just cringe when I think about how I used to act when I was using. I just thought I was so cool. I went to bed with a lot of girls. It was like a game. I didn't really care about any of them. It was just for my own ego, you know.

"I got one girl pregnant and totally blew her off. She ended up having to get an abortion all by herself and paid for the whole thing herself too. Can you imagine how awful that must have been? To be alone like that? I was just a total asshole and my friends supported this, you know. They were just as bad as I was.

"I don't know what I can do now to make amends. I feel so bad, but that's not enough. I just don't know what to do next."

Joyce:

"My whole life I've only had one relationship. I went out with the same guy for three years. That's it, only one.

"We broke up and now I just want to stay out of any kind of relationship for a while. I'm not sure that I even want to go out with anyone for a long, long time.

"I have mixed feelings — part of me feels rejected if I don't get any male attention, and I definitely don't want to be like that, but part of me is more secure with myself and I just want time to be me. Part of me also dreads the thought of another long-term commitment."

Chad:

"I told myself that the first time I have sex, I'm not going to be messed up and it's going to be with somebody I've been going out with for a while. As it happened, this came true, so I didn't even feel guilty. I had been going out with her for five months.

"Having sex was nothing great, but afterwards we just laid there and talked — that was the cool part. You know, she's the only person I've ever done that with. Every other time I've been drunk.

"The other people I slept with when I was using — I couldn't call them the next day. I felt too guilty to call them. I'd wake up the next day and know it was wrong, you know. My morals about sex are completely opposite to what I did. I don't think it's right to have sex with somebody if you don't love them. That's my moral, and because I broke it so many times, I'd wake up the next day and feel real down about myself.

"I wasn't proud of it at all. It was just total self-gratification when it happened. Afterward it was like *Shit. I hope my friends don't find out.*"

So, What's My Sex Life Going to be Like Now?

Now comes the tough part. You're straight and you want to stay that way, so that means you may want to make some decisions about your sexuality up front.

115

I promise not to start lecturing on morality. I'm only suggesting that now is the time to decide what kind of sexual lifestyle you want for yourself. Don't wait until after the urge hits you. (You know how *that* can fog your thinking.)

Some sponsors and treatment counselors recommend that you don't engage in any sexual relations for at least six months to a year. That might sound harsh, but healing from the physical and emotional damage drugs cause takes a different amount of time for different people. It doesn't hurt to wait until your thoughts and feelings have come more into focus — until you're feeling like you're starting to know yourself sober — before you leap into a sexual relationship. But when it comes right down to it, the decision is yours. So what are some of your choices?

- Abstinence — no sex, no way, no how.
- Sexual relations only after you've gone out with someone for a while and fallen madly in love with them.

Don't wait until after the urge hits you.

- Sexual relations only after you've known someone long enough to know their last name.

And that's just to name a few. You need to figure what's right for you. You know what your sexual lifestyle was like when you were using. How would you like it to be different?

If you weren't practicing birth control when you were using, that will become a *must* if you're sexually active. Maybe you'll choose to become sexually active only after you're sure about a relationship. Or maybe you will decide to abstain from sex for a while.

It's likely that you'll want your sexual lifestyle to be different from when you were using. If you find someone you want to become sexually involved with, ask yourself:

- How well do I know this person?
- How will sex change the relationship?
- How will I feel the next day?
- Will it affect my sobriety?
- Am I protected from sexually-transmitted diseases or unwanted pregnancy?
- What are my reasons for wanting to go to bed with this person?
- Is having sex with this person in line with the values I've set for myself?

These questions aren't designed to make sex a chore or to take the fun out of it, but to give you a chance to really think about what you're getting into.

Most of us already have too many regrets from our using days, so putting some thought into what we want our sexuality to be, up front, will help us avoid adding more regrets.

How to Avoid Sex Shame

Why is there so much guilt and shame associated with sex? For most of us, there are two main reasons.

1. We may have been taught to think that certain acts or thoughts are "sinful" or "dirty."

117

2. The way we have acted sexually may not match our values — the way we would like to be.

What Are Your Sexual Values?

Ask yourself how you really feel about all of the different aspects of your sexuality. Maybe, when you were younger, you were taught that some things are not okay and you really think they are okay. Or maybe there are some things society accepts as okay and you don't accept as okay.

Take time to explore your thoughts and feelings about your sexuality. Find out what feels right for you. Remember, your sexual attitudes aren't necessarily constant. They may change and grow as you do. Decide what values are comfortable for you now.

Decide What Your Sexual Behavior Will Be

If your sexual behavior is in conflict with your sexual attitudes and values, you will feel guilty. To avoid that, your sexual behavior needs to match your sense of what's right.

Sometimes, even though you may be acting in line with your beliefs, you may feel shame about your sexuality. This shame may come from old messages that people have given you about sex. You will know by the way you feel if your behavior matches your values.

Also, if someone wants you to do something that you're not comfortable with, you need to say no. Doing something you don't feel comfortable with will only make you feel bad. Your first concern should be to yourself and your sobriety.

It's hard to talk about sexual values without making sex sound like work. Believe me, that's not my intention. Sex can be fun, playful, stimulating, lusty, enjoyable, fulfilling, and satisfying *when it's at the right time and with the right person.* And when it's not? Well, then it's a drag to put it mildly.

The people I know seem to have two things in common: (1) now that they're straight, they feel like they have choices, and (2) they've not only thought about what *they* want, but are talking about their concerns and feelings to each other.

Janine:

"When I got out of treatment, I said to myself, *I'm not going to go out with or go to bed with anyone for six months.*

"After a month, I met a guy at NA that I really liked. I wanted to go out with him and I didn't know what to do. When he asked me out, I turned him down and, surprisingly, I felt pretty good about my decision.

119

"I just told him I'm not going out with anyone for a while. I know I was doing what was best for *me* for a change. I was putting myself first and not allowing my life to be complicated by a guy.

"I don't know if I'll make it six months. I just take it One Day at a Time."

Michael:

"I've never had a relationship that's lasted more than a couple of weeks. I'm scared to start one now, but I don't want what I had before either.

"I think I just need some friends right now — both male and female."

Tammy:

"I still get insecure when it comes to men, but I feel more secure with myself than before. A lot of it comes with self-esteem. If you have a good self-esteem, it doesn't matter how much you weigh, what kind of makeup you're wearing, how well your hair is styled, or what clothing you're wearing — all that doesn't matter if you're secure. One friend of mine says all the time, 'It's not the package, it's what's inside.' "

LeAnn:

"I feel good about my sexuality now. I know it's okay to get sexually excited about someone. I don't always have to act on it, but when I do, I don't have to be ashamed either."

Patrick:

"I hardly went out with anyone when I was using. I'm kind of shy and I've always been afraid of rejection.

"I'm going out with someone now and it's neat, you know? We've been together for four months and I've never been able to talk to anyone like I can talk to her.

"We didn't do anything sexually until about two months ago. It's really different for both of us; it's a time when we can feel closer, but we're not like obsessed with it, and we're responsible with birth control. It's great."

Jackie:

"I'm really protective of my sexuality now. I date once in a while, but I haven't gone out with anyone I care to get serious about.

"Even at AA meetings, I don't think I should *have* to hug any guy who approaches me. You kind of feel like a bitch at first, but I don't want to ever feel like I can't say no. You know, I'm just honest about when I feel uncomfortable.

"I have a few male friends, but most of my friends now are women. I think I respect myself more now.

"I'm sure I sound totally paranoid or stuck on myself, but it's not like that. It's just a matter of trying to put myself first."

Todd:

"I think I've outgrown some things since I've gone straight, like porno. After you've seen it once, the novelty kind of wears off. The stuff is pretty degrading to women. They're twisted into humiliating positions and basically seen as just a hole for sex. I'm not into it. I just want to be around real women.

"Some of the guys who come into the program get a lot of their identity through sex — you know, like

121

the more you got it, the better you are. When they go straight, they think that unless they're getting laid every night there's something wrong with them, like that's what makes them a man.

"I don't care who you are or how long you've been straight, if you don't handle sex in a mature way and deal with your feelings, you're going to slip. If you feel nervous, scared, rejected, or ashamed, you got to talk to the person about it. If you keep it inside, you're going to start getting high again."

Karen:

"Right now I am bound and determined not to sleep with anybody until I care about them and they care about me back. That's going to be a big step for me. Last year was the first time I've slept with somebody and not felt totally guilty, which is another step in the right direction.

"I feel good that I haven't had to build my self-esteem on the fact that men will like me or my body. I feel good and I'm not about to give that up."

How to Love Your Body (Imperfections and All) In Five Easy Lessons

Your sexuality is all tied up with your self-image, which is usually all tied up with how you feel about your body. Here are some tips on how to feel good about it.

Lesson #1 *Treat Yourself Right*

- *Don't use anything with the drug nicotine in it.* Nicotine is one of the most highly addictive drugs, and cigarettes, which contain nicotine, kill more people every year than all other drugs combined.

122

- *Eat healthy foods.* Eat a lot of whole grains, fruits, and vegetables. Go easy on meat, dairy products, sugar, and fat. Get at least three balanced meals a day, don't stuff yourself, and cut out the late night snacks. (I swear, I'm starting to sound like my mother.)

- *Get a half hour of exercise at least three times a week.* This could include swimming, skiing, biking, walking, tennis, basketball . . . you get the picture.

Lesson #2 *Forget What the Rest of the World Thinks*

Let's face it, we're surrounded by images of what we are "supposed" to look like. Everywhere we turn there are "beautiful bodies" staring back at us from billboards, TV shows, magazines, and movies. It's no wonder that we may start to feel inadequate, especially when the only images that the media presents us with are images of somebody else's idea of perfection.

The best thing you can do to combat this is create your own image of what you think is attractive. I remember one young people's AA meeting: the room was filled with young women, but what was strange was that they all had long hair with their bangs spiked out — all except for one. She had short hair, very simple, and no hair spray. Her face was what often gets described as average looking, yet she was stunning — she stood out. The lesson I learned from her is this: don't be afraid to create your own style, your own image.

Lesson #3 *You Are What You Feel*

I know this is easy to say, but it really works: *If you feel attractive on the inside, people will find you attractive on the outside.*

I told the story about the young woman who created her own style to a guy I know and he said, "Sure, I can create my own style that I think looks cool, but what if no one else does?"

Trust me, the people who matter to you will. Otherwise, apply Lesson #2!

123

When you let others decide for you what a "good" body is and isn't, you end up with a big dose of self-hatred. When you feel bad about yourself and are constantly putting yourself down, you probably are not helping yourself reach your goal of being a confident, self-assured individual. So start giving yourself some positive messages about your body.

No matter what your body looks like, you can start feeling good about it. Maybe your stomach is a little round, but maybe it's kind of sexy that way. Maybe your back is scrawny, but in perfect proportion to the rest of your body. You don't have to fit a mold of what's attractive. You have your own special features. Start to fall in love with yourself.

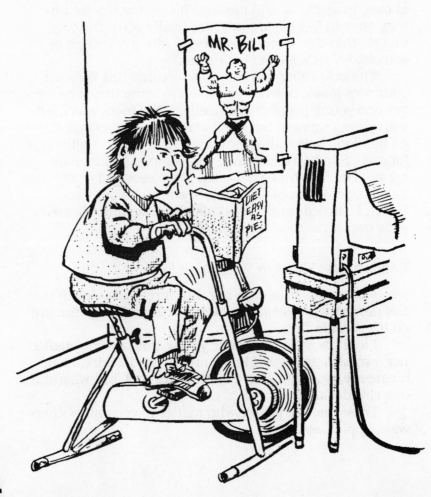

Lesson #4 *Know If Food Is an Obsession with You*

If you think in any way that you may be abusing food by compulsive overeating, bingeing and purging, or starving yourself, please seek help. Eating disorders, especially bulimia and anorexia, are very serious. If you think you have a problem, please look into a self-help group or check your local hospital for information on where to find help. Do it right away.

Lesson #5 *Don't Expect Perfection*

It's impossible to follow any plan perfectly. It's equally impossible to feel good about ourselves every day of the year, but that's okay, we don't have to. We all have our good days and bad days.

Sometimes I think, *I'm going to work out really hard and diet and get to looking really good. Then, I won't have to worry about any of this stuff.* What usually happens is that I feel miserable because I can't live up to the standards and regimen I've set for myself.

We have to remind ourselves that we don't need to fit someone else's idea of beauty. We can treat our body with respect and love — inside and out.

Talking About Sexuality
With Your Friends

Cory:

"I was always so worried about whether or not I was satisfying the girl I was with, but then I'd get so wasted that I didn't care. Even when I did care, I was too chicken to ask.

"Now I feel good that my girlfriend and I can enjoy sex and have fun, and it doesn't have to be just sex. We give back rubs and it feels good just being close."

125

Talking about sexuality will usually stir a lot of interest.

April:

"One thing that was so taboo to talk about before going straight was masturbation. One night a bunch of us were talking and the subject came up. I couldn't believe it, but everybody had done it at one time or another. Not just the guys either. It was like, *You're kidding, you mean I'm not some kind of pervert.* Everyone was so matter-of-fact about it. Then, we made a bunch of jokes about having hair on our palms and going blind and stuff like that. I think everyone was a little relieved.

"There's so much guilt associated with masturbation from church and everything. It's so stupid 'cause it's really a normal part of growing up. Now, I think it's okay. It's not sinful or anything."

Michelle:

"I'm honest about what I like and what I don't like. If I don't want to have sex, I'll say 'Jon, let's not have sex today.' With my other boyfriends, I was afraid of hurting their feelings.

"I'm more comfortable with my body, with my period too. It's like I can be comfortable around Jon when I'm naked."

Tyler:

"It seems like just about anything dealing with sex is easier to talk about now that I'm straight. Even stuff that's totally embarrassing, like hard-ons and stuff like that. Me and these two guys were talking about not being able to last very long during sex, you know, getting off too soon. Anyway, it was nice to hear other guys saying that it was tough for them, too, instead of hearing all that macho bullshit. We're not a bunch of sex maniacs or anything. We don't talk about sex all the time. In fact, I wouldn't talk to just anybody about it either, because you feel stupid sometimes. But when it does come up, now I can talk about it better."

Lindsey:

"One of the first guys I got involved with after treatment turned out to be a total ass. I started to figure this all out once we started having sex. He was really into oral sex and I was really not. I've tried it before with other guys, but I think it's totally gross and it's not fun for me in the least. Anyway, he tried to guilt me into it, you know, the 'if you really loved me' crap. Needless to say, we broke up.

"Afterwards, I felt kind of inadequate, like maybe I should have done it, so I talked to other girls about it and they said that they felt the same way and that I should be proud of myself for being honest, because a lot of girls would have just done it and put their own feelings second."

127

The Basics in Making
Good Choices About Sex

If you are going to be sexually active and you don't want to become pregnant, you or your partner must practice some form of birth control.

Sometimes, young women think they can't get pregnant or that they are infertile. Infertility is extremely rare in young women. In fact, half of all initial premarital pregnancies occur in the first six months of sexual activity. It can happen to you!

And pulling out is NOT a form of birth control, nor is the rhythm method very effective. Your best bet is to go to a Planned Parenthood clinic near you to discuss your options. They will help you choose among reliable birth control options that match your lifestyle.

A visit there is confidential — no one has to find out — and cost is minimal (or nothing if you can't afford to pay). Males are welcome too. In fact, you may feel more comfortable getting condoms there than your local drugstore.

The decision to be sexually active carries responsibilities — with potentially damaging consequences if ignored.

AIDS and Other Sexually Transmitted Diseases

Well, I think I know what most of you think about this topic: *It's not going to happen to me.*

I don't know what to say to make it clear that it really *can* happen to you.

At this time, there are over one million people infected with the AIDS virus in the United States, a number that I'm sure will be outdated soon after this book is published. And the incidence of AIDS among young people is growing. That means you.

AIDS isn't all you have to worry about when you're careless about sex. Herpes, gonorrhea, and syphilis are still around too. The only way to be 100 percent safe is to abstain from sex . If you're not going to do that, the next best thing is to make sure that you or your partner *always* wears a condom.

Being sober doesn't mean just not using or drinking, it means living our life on new terms. We're responsible for our decisions, and safe sex is another way we show we care about ourselves and the people around us.

There's More to Intimacy than Sex

Couples I've talked to who are really satisfied with their sex life often admit that they don't need to have sex very often. One young woman put it this way, "It's really strange, but it seems like the times we feel closest is when we're doing something like hiking or reading, you know, something totally unrelated to sex."

Her partner chimed in, "It's true. I used to think that the only way to show affection was to be fooling around every night, but now it's more like we're friends. We have so much fun together."

Our culture puts so much emphasis on sex that sometimes it's easy to forget that it's really a very small part of a relationship.

Developing true intimacy with someone comes from sharing and learning about each other — from discovering things about your partner's family background, beliefs, dreams, and goals, and by celebrating your similarities and differences.

When you've built a friendship based on mutual respect, sex becomes the natural expression of caring that helps to make a relationship intimate.

Sexual Orientation

Treatment is often the first time that people who are attracted to members of the same sex are able to open up and talk about it. One young person described it this way, "It's like finding out that your whole life you've been forcing yourself to write with your left hand and then you realize that it's much more natural to use your right hand."

So where does sexual or affectional preference come from? Well, this can get a bit complicated. It's normal for heterosexual people to be attracted to or experiment sexually with people of the same sex, and it's normal for homosexual people to be attracted to or experiment with heterosexual relationships. Of course, some people consider themselves bisexual, which means being sexually attracted to both sexes. Whatever your preference, almost everyone agrees that it's possible to know your sexual or affectional preference from a very early age.

Melody:

> "I remember feeling different ever since I was real little — maybe four or five. I guess it hit me the hardest a few years later when all the other girls in my class were really going gaga over boys. I didn't feel the same way."

Once the News Is Out

If you are gay or lesbian, you may be just beginning to open up about it as you sober up. Often, the fear and shame around this part of yourself has played a part in your chemical abuse. Recovery means getting in touch with yourself and accepting and loving yourself for who you are — something that you may not have allowed yourself to do before.

Recovery won't make everything a bed of roses, of course. As any gay person already knows, there are many obstacles to feeling accepted in our society.

As totally unfair and senseless as it seems, homophobia — an irrational fear of homosexuality — is not going to go away, not for a while anyway. The obstacles you'll encounter may be found in your own family, and certainly in the community at large.

Lack of Family Support

When you're not being shamed by subtle and not so subtle hurtful comments, you may face a wall of denial in your family, with no one willing to talk about your sexual lifestyle. Most families wouldn't encourage you to bring your partner home for the holidays or for family gatherings.

Bob:

> "I was invited to a cousin's wedding and the invitation was addressed to me and 'guest'. I really wanted to bring Tom. We had been seeing each other for over a year and I wanted my family to accept us. Well, my parents just about had a fit!

Suddenly these people who were supposedly so supportive of me were wondering what people would think. I was so pissed. If I had been going out with a woman that long, it would have been no problem. I brought him anyway and it went really good. There were a few rough spots, but it went pretty good. I think my folks were surprised.

"God, I don't know what they thought I was going to do, walk up to people and say, 'This is Tom. We sleep together.'"

Discrimination in Your Community

If you are gay or lesbian, you may encounter discrimination on the job or in trying to find housing. For example, you may be passed over for new jobs or promotions, or fired from the job you have. Or you may be mysteriously denied an apartment you're perfectly qualified to rent. The worst part is that in most areas of the country, there are no laws protecting you.

In fact, there are a lot of laws still on the books that actually restrict your rights. One you'll find in just about every state is the restriction of marriage licenses to gay and lesbian couples.

In nearly everything you see — most movies, magazines, books, advertising, and television — promotes only the heterosexual lifestyle as normal. Whether you're in high school facing the ridicule of your peers, or out in the world where public shows of affection may draw anything from condemning frowns to outright violence, coming out will present you with major challenges to your self-esteem and serenity.

Just about everywhere you go,
only one lifestyle is promoted.

Sounding Pretty Grim?

It's a lot to deal with, but denying how you feel or trying to become something you're not isn't the answer. It's important to come to terms with who you are, how you feel, and accept yourself. Whether through the support of your Higher Power, an affirming support group, a sensitive counselor, or some combination, you don't have to be alone.

Many young people find that joining a gay/lesbian rights group helps a lot too. Working to change society's attitudes and the laws that discriminate against gays and lesbians can build a sense of community and purpose.

Curt:

"All through high school I dated the same girl. When I went into treatment, she was real supportive and went to all the family groups and stuff. And then I dropped the big bomb — I'm gay. I felt really bad for her, it was a total shock.

"Treatment kind of went downhill from there too. The guys in my group didn't really want to have anything to do with me. There were two people on the whole unit that I could talk to. I started to wonder if I should have just kept quiet.

"Then my counselor got in touch with two guys from the gay men's AA meeting in town and had them come up and talk to me. It helped a lot!

"Since I've been out, I feel like I've got a whole new family. I've met so many new people and I have a whole new network of friends.

"I guess I would like to say to anyone who's gay and who's in treatment right now to work your program and make contact with other gay people in the program and the rest will fall into place."

Jessie:

"My parents had a terrible time dealing with it. You know, parents don't want to imagine that their kids ever have sex with *anyone*. I mean you could be fifty-three and have five kids and they still don't want to imagine you having sex, but if you tell them you're lesbian, sex is the first thing that pops into their mind.

"I'm in a relationship right now and it's not like we fool around all day. I mean, we have lives. It's just like any other relationship. When people hear the word 'gay' or 'lesbian,' though, that's what they think.

"I'm so thankful for my sobriety because it's given me an opportunity to quit numbing out and to enjoy life. My parents are better now, but anyone who can't deal with me — that's their problem, not mine."

Ron:

"If I wasn't straight, I'd probably be dead right now. I always had so much shame over how I felt, I probably would have committed suicide or got into a car accident or who knows?"

"I can't believe I'm even the same person. I see *everything* so different now. I'm truly happy."

Sara:

"I guess I would just encourage anyone who's gay to get involved with some organizations like the International Gay and Lesbian Youth Organization, Act Up, or any university group. They give you a place to fit in and a way to 'fight the system' if you want. Definitely check them out."

Tim:

"You're going to run into a lot of shit out there — people calling you 'fag' to your face and shit like that. Even people who think they're so liberal say things like 'Geez, it's too bad you're gay. I guess you'll have to make the best of it.'

"Staying straight is the only way to deal with it. I'm not going to lose my sobriety over someone else's ignorance. At least that way my life won't go down the toilet."

Being gay or lesbian means that you are going to run into obstacles that other people don't have to deal with. The best way to overcome them is to make your sobriety the most important thing in your life. With your program as a foundation, you'll be able to take the rest as it comes, twenty-four hours at a time.

Sexual Victimization

Sexual victimization isn't about sexuality, it's about power and domination. Unfortunately, it's very common. According to one study, one out of every six boys and one out of every four girls are sexually assaulted by age eighteen. The numbers may be even higher because so much abuse goes unreported — especially among males.

If you are a victim of sexual assault, you *can* survive and go on with your life, but you'll eventually need to deal with the pain and anger. Getting high will only postpone your healing.

If you are a victim of sexual assault, you don't have to block it out by getting high.

What Is Sexual Assault?

When we think of incest (sexual contact between members of the same family) and sexual assault, child molestation and rape are usually what come to mind.

But sexual assault does not necessarily involve violence or physical force. If someone threatens you if you don't have sex with them, or if you have sex with them because you're afraid of what they'll do if you don't, you are a victim of sexual assault.

Sexual assault occurs when someone touches you in a sexual way on any area of your body that you didn't want them to touch. This may include your genitals, buttocks, thighs, chest, or breasts. It's assault if they touch you with their hands, mouth, genitals, or an object.

The Offender

A sexual offender is rarely the stereotypical weird old man in a trench coat. Most victims of sexual assault know the offender, who is often someone they trusted, like a relative, friend of the family, co-worker, or date. Studies consistently show that whether the victim is male or female, the vast majority of offender are heterosexual males. That is why so many of the stories in this section are about heterosexual male offenders.

Even if the stories in this chapter don't describe exactly what happened to you, you may still identify with the victims' feelings. Victims of sexual assault may have many feelings about the assault and they are usually very mixed up. The most common feelings are *anger* at the offender and *shame* from victims blaming themselves for the assault. Victims of sexual assault often have to work to realize that *it was not their fault.* A victim may think, *I shouldn't have gone with him,* or *I should have fought harder,* or *I shouldn't have been dressed that way.* Some victims may think, *You don't know my situation; it really was my fault.*

It's easy for an assault victim to try to find ways to blame him- or herself because he or she may think, *If I can figure out what I did wrong before, I can prevent it from happening again.* But the fact is, sexual assault can happen to anyone. If someone violates you, it is *their*

138

fault, not yours. Even if you were on a date and said yes to your date's advances, but then changed your mind and said no — no means no. No matter what the situation, no one deserves to be assaulted.

Mary:

"The guy who raped me couldn't have cared in the least what he did to me. He didn't even think he did anything wrong.

"I went out with him, and when it came to the end of the evening, he figured I owed him something. He thought I was saying no as part of a game. I was crying, yelling. There was nothing I could do.

"Then, the worst was yet to come. I went to a therapist thinking that I would get some help and he assaulted me too.

"I finally got in contact with a victims' center where I was able to talk to other women who'd been through what I'd been through. I had so much anger. I still have anger . . . I think it's good for me to hang on to some of it because it keeps me helping other victims and fighting for better laws."

Tracy:

"My dad molested me from the time I was five until about fifteen. It's so hard for me to talk about it. I feel like he took part of me.

"I have bad days — days where I just feel so down, but most of the time I just try to get on with my life, you know, he may have ruined a big portion of my life, but he's not going to ruin the rest."

Christopher:

"For a long time after it happened, I tried to go to bed with every girl I came in contact with. It was

139

like I was trying to prove my manhood or something, 'cause I couldn't figure out why this guy
picked me. I didn't know if I was gay or what.

"I know now that he could have picked anybody."

Jody:

"I was at a party one night and I was totally
wasted. Anyway, this guy I liked brought me
upstairs to this bedroom and we started making
out. We were really getting into it. I don't know
how long we were there when I realized that a
bunch of his buddies had come into the room.

"I didn't know what to do. I got scared right away.
I couldn't really move or think. I was just para-
lyzed. I remember saying 'What the hell's going
on?' and I heard one of them say 'We're going to
have some fun.'

"They all raped me. Sometimes there was more
than one guy on me at a time. I couldn't do a
damn thing to stop it.

"The next day I was feeling everything — anger,
shame, humiliation. I talked to a friend of our
family who is a lawyer and she said the guys
would probably never even get probation because
it would be my word against theirs and I was
wasted. These guys were supposed to be my
friends! I just felt like dirt — like a piece of shit.

"Since this happened to me, I found out that
something like one out of every four rapes involves
more than one rapist.

"Even though I'm not in partying situations anymore, I don't feel safe. I don't think I'll ever feel
safe. Women just don't have the same life as men.
We just can't walk anywhere we want to. It's like
we live in a war zone.

"I just am glad to be straight and to be getting my life back together. Using would just make me feel worse."

Maria:

"When I was little, my parents always told me to watch out for strangers and stuff like that. Well they never told me to watch out for my aunt.

"When someone molests or rapes you, people think you should just 'get over it.' It's just not that easy. You think about it all the time. It takes years and years to forget, so sometimes you've got to feel bad about it. It's not like you can snap your fingers and get over it. But you don't have to let it control your whole life either."

Jordon:

"I don't know how to explain how I felt. I guess I felt scared and helpless. What was so confusing, though, was that I also felt sexually stimulated. I have a hard time talking about it. It's just that, you know, certain areas of the body can be sexually stimulated and so you feel like it's your fault that this happened and that you liked it or something. But inside, everything feels like crap. It messed me up for a long time. The guy who did it never got sent to jail or anything either.

"Nowadays, I try to focus my attention on other things. I work on my sobriety. I don't need to get high to cover my feelings anymore."

Mary Kay:

"I was attacked by a guy I work with, after I was straight for a while.

"I was physically ill after it happened — throwing up and stuff. I had to quit my job because he was there. I couldn't stand to be anywhere — not even at my house. Every little noise scared me.

"I didn't want to be around any men. Not my boyfriend, not at NA, nowhere.

"I wanted to use bad, but instead I just talked. I talk about it all the time, to anyone who'll listen. It's been about seven months and I'm just starting to feel normal again."

Mary:

"For a long time, I used the attack as an excuse to get loaded — a damn good excuse I might add, but still an excuse. Now I stay straight for myself because I deserve better."

What's the Next Step?

If you were sexually assaulted, make sure you keep your program for sobriety on track and stay straight. During any crisis in your life, you are especially prone to relapse. Keep doing the things that work for you — meetings, readings, contact with other straight people, counseling — whatever it takes.

Often, when people first go straight, they think it's necessary to right away start dealing with all of the past crises in their lives. They may have been told by other well-meaning recovering people and counselors that if they don't deal with it right now, they are never going to be able to stay straight.

That's not always true. Your first priority is to get sober. You're not going to be able to deal with anything if your thoughts and feelings are run by your addiction. If you feel you're not ready to talk about or deal with some things right way, don't.

Taking Back Your Power

If you were victimized by sexual assault, all of your power and control was taken away by the offender. When you start to face your addiction, you have already begun to take back some of your power and control. (Powerlessness in Step One applies to your addiction, not necessarily to the other parts of your life.) Maybe you'll find that you really do need to talk about what happened right away, but maybe you won't. If you want to concentrate only on your sobriety for the first year and wait to deal with other issues, that's okay.

By the same token, it's important to realize that when you're ready to talk about what happened, talking does help the pain go away. Sometimes an assault can have a lot of power over you because you may keep reliving it and building it up in your mind. Breaking the silence about what happened can be the first step toward releasing some of its power. Each time you talk about it, you'll feel its grip on you slipping away.

When you decide that you're ready to talk, it's important to do so in a safe environment. Here are some places you can contact for support.

- *A sexual assault or rape crisis center.* Most cities have one. Check your phone book. Often, they will have self-help and support groups and many other services.
- *A counselor.* Ask people you trust if they know of a good counselor. If your community has a sexual assault center or something similar, they can refer you to someone who specializes in this area. It's best to find someone who's comfortable dealing with sexual abuse issues. Most important, you should be comfortable with who you're seeing.
- *A victim's action group.* See if there's a victim's action group available in your area that fights to change the laws that make it difficult to prosecute rapists. Being a part of a group like this can help you feel like you have some power to change the world. A sexual assault center may be able to tell you if there's such a group in your area.

Reporting the Assault

You may or may not decide to report to the police what happened to you. How to handle this is totally up to you. You are not a bad person if you decide not to report it. You know what you can and can't deal with. Often, getting involved with the legal system can make you feel like a victim all over again.

On the other hand, pressing charges can be a way of taking back your power and control. If you decide to go this route, I would highly recommend asking for help from a sexual assault or rape crisis center. Even if there is not one in your area, call the closest one. They will tell you what you can expect and will walk you through the system.

One last thing about crisis centers: in some states there are mandatory reporting laws, which means that if you were under the age of eighteen at the time of the assault and you give them your last name, they are required by law to report the crime to the police. (In a

144

few states, Minnesota, for example, this is true only in cases of incest.) So you know where you stand, it's very important to ask the people you talk to at a crisis center if the law applies to your situation. They will be honest with you and offer you services anyway. They are there to help you.

For Offenders

If you are an offender, chances are that reading this won't cause you to admit that you've got a problem. But it is very, very important that you eventually get some help. Your need to have power and control over others is not going to just go away. Even if you are straight and working a Twelve Step program, you're going to have to do the additional work of becoming responsible for your actions. Otherwise, you're setting yourself up for relapse and the probability of hurting somebody else.

Call a sexual assault center. No one is going to throw you in jail. Explain your situation and ask them for names of reliable counselors.

Educate yourself. Read everything you can about oppression and the effects of violence. Just being willing to do these things means you have a chance at changing your behavior and attitudes.

The Complex Problem of Sexual Assault and Chemical Dependency

Many victims of sexual assault started abusing chemicals only after the sexual assault. Until then, they may have used or drank only moderately with no adverse consequences.

If this is the case with you, you may have some doubt in your mind as to whether or not you are chemically dependent — and it's possible you're not. Abusing alcohol or other drugs is the way some victims deal with the trauma of sexual assault. There are no easy answers and there will probably always be some controversy surrounding the issue, but one statement can be made pretty safely, *continued chemical use will not help your situation.*

Even if you do not think you're alcoholic or addicted to other drugs, staying straight for a while is still a good idea. Give yourself some time. Take it a day at a time and maybe after you've been sober awhile (up to a year or more for many), you'll have had an opportunity to deal with the assault and get a better feeling of the role chemicals played in your life.

CHAPTER 6

Relationships, *Or* All Those People We Hate to Love and Love To Hate

Lesson One: Nothing More than Feelings

Okay, class, heads up, eyes to the front. Pay attention. We are going to do a little simple arithmetic. Ready?

A Person + Another Person = _____

Anyone know the answer? Anyone? Relationship? Yes, that's right, but what happens when you have a relationship, class? Feelings! Very good. Two people and a relationship equals feelings. Can you say *pain and anguish*, boys and girls? How about *love and ecstasy*? Can you say *roller coaster of emotions*?

Lesson Two: Feeling Better May Seem to Feel Worse

I know you've heard it a million times before: Alcoholism is the "feelings" disease. Well, it really is.

It seems much easier to use drugs than to feel. And addicts use so they don't have to feel. Got an ache, got a pain? Have I got a pill for you. Eventually, though, we

147

found out the hard way that chemicals weren't the solution. We figured out that when we came out of our stupor, we still had all our old aches and pains, and a few more.

When you decide to lead a straight life and work the program, you are also choosing to deal with your emotions instead of getting high. Maybe you've already discovered it's not as bad as you thought it would be.

When talking about relationships, I don't mean only that special love, I mean anyone we have feelings toward and who affects how we feel about ourselves, including friends, employers, co-workers, parents, siblings, and other relatives. So let's talk about feelings. (Now, how do you feel about that?)

The Good Stuff First

Love, happiness, excitement, joy — feeling good. Feeling good doesn't give most people much trouble — it's feeling bad they don't like. But there are some traps a lot of us alcoholics and addicts get into that make good feelings as hard to deal with as painful ones.

Many of us actually feel guilty if we feel too good. It's like we catch ourselves and think, *Oh no, I should be working on myself. I should be rooting out all my defects, not having fun.*

We may feel like we don't deserve to have fun or that we should be constantly striving for perfection — which means being constantly disappointed.

Staying clean and sober means learning to have *fun!* Feeling good, getting our adrenalin flowing, and having fun can take the place of the high we were looking for with drugs. Except this high lasts, and it comes from simply being alive.

Of course, we need to face our problems and deal with them as they happen. When we get in the habit of doing that daily, we do the work and then are free to have fun and feel good about it. To get into the habit, you may need to take some time each day and label it "worry-free" time and refuse to be brought down for that period. If you want, you can promise yourself that you'll start feeling bad as soon as the time runs out.

Lindsey:

"I know this is going to sound fake, but it seems like I practically never feel bad anymore. I can't believe it myself. You know, it's like I keep waiting for something to go wrong, or I'll sit and concentrate on my feelings and think maybe I'm being phony and just covering up. I used to live with all of this major conflict in my life when I was using, but now I honestly feel great."

Janet:

"After I was straight for about five months, I got this job I wanted for so long. I had to go through two interviews and pass a test to get it. I was just flying when they called to tell me I got it. I was at home by myself kind of letting it sink in when I got an urge to get high. It was really weird. I was feeling really content and I just thought, *You know what would even feel better? If I'd smoke a joint.*

"I started thinking about how great it was when I first started getting high. I ended up calling a friend of mine from NA and talking about it. Once I talked it through, I was okay, but it was scary for me to think that the urge could be so powerful even when I was feeling good."

Matt:

"I take it for granted when I feel good, and I forget to tell people when they help make me feel good. What I mean is, it's easy to know when someone pisses you off, but saying 'I feel great when I'm around you' is a totally different thing for me."

Now Comes the Hard Part

Like it or not, we all have negative emotions. Staying straight means dealing with these feelings in a different way than when we were using. Easy to say, right?

Anger, Resentment, and Hate

Ah yes, anger, resentment, and hate — three of the staples in life for alcoholics and addicts. As you might guess, these three emotions are very closely related. Resentment is anger held onto and hatred is anger made extreme. So let's talk about anger.

When you become angry, it usually means that someone did something that you think was unfair or didn't do something that you think they should have. Basically, what you are saying is: *If they would just be more like I want them to be, the world would be a better place.*

Many people think it's bad to feel anger, or any negative emotion for that matter. This is not at all what I believe. Anger can motivate us to take positive action. Anger can move us to work to change injustices in the world. We can't help the way we feel; it just happens. Feeling isn't negative or positive, but the way we deal with a feeling like anger — or any feeling — can be positive or negative.

If they would just be more like I want them to be . . .

Jack:

"At school the other day, this kid I used to get high with started giving me shit about something stupid I said in class. He's a total jerk and I don't like him anyway, so I was set off right away.

"When I was using, I probably would have gotten into it with him. I'm sure we would have probably ended up fighting and getting detention or something.

151

"Anyway, I ended up walking away from him feeling stupid and not saying anything. Later, after talking to some people about it, I decided to confront him. I told him that I felt stupid about what I said in class and that I didn't appreciate his comments. He was still kind of a jerk. I know I caught him off guard, but I know I did the right thing, too, because now I'm over it.

"Looking back, I can think of a lot of ways I could have dealt with the situation. You know, I could have felt sorry for myself and got loaded; I could have told him I was embarrassed and asked him to knock it off; I could have punched him out; I could have blown him off all together and decided he wasn't worth my time; I could have laughed right along with him — the list goes on and on. I just know now that I can start dealing with my feelings without being an ass and without using."

. . . don't discount your anger by telling yourself that you're not angry.

152

If you are mad at someone and you continually choose to ignore or stuff your anger, there's a good chance that it will build into resentment and then hate. This is a good way to set yourself up to relapse. You are better off dealing with it. Dealing with your anger doesn't always mean confronting the person you're angry at, but it does mean not hanging on to it.

There are no quick fixes, but there are three questions you can ask yourself before you decide to act (or not act) on your anger.

Question #1 *What Am I Angry About?*

Once you realize that you are mad at someone, don't discount it by telling yourself that you're not angry. Accept it. Then ask yourself what you are angry about.

For instance, if a friend of mine, Mike, is supposed to pick me up at the library and he is forty-five minutes late, I'll probably be upset. Why? Because it seems to me that he's being either irresponsible or doesn't care about my feelings. *My feelings are important, I deserve consideration* is the positive message I'm giving myself by being upset.

Question #2 *Have I Considered All the Angles?*

It's important to do this, not so you can talk yourself out of being angry, but so you can get a handle on the whole situation. Answering this question will help you to decide what to do next.

For example, while waiting at the library for Mike to pick me up, I might remember that he has been really busy and had said that a job interview might cause him to be late. Or I might realize that my anger is partially due to not getting much sleep and feeling crabby about other things.

When looking at all the angles, you may think of a dozen good reasons why you shouldn't be angry, but still are. You may still feel upset no matter how reasonable the other person's behavior appears. If you are still mad, be willing to admit it to yourself and find someone you feel comfortable talking it out with.

Question #3 *What Am I Going to Do About It?*

You have two options: (1) don't confront the person with your feelings, or (2) confront them.

In the situation with Mike, I may decide not to confront him, because after thinking it through, I may realize I'm not angry with him anymore, or that much of my anger was carried over from something else.

Choosing Not to Confront the Person

Sometimes you will choose not to confront someone because you figure it won't do any good anyway. Maybe you've already talked to the person about the same problem many times before and didn't get anywhere. But if after deciding not to confront the person you are still upset, you need to do something about it.

To cool off, you may need to

- talk to someone — a friend, your sponsor, someone from your support group.
- work within the system — file a grievance if it's a work issue or report it if it's a legal issue.
- work outside of the system — by protest or petition if the situation warrants it.
- work it through by yourself — meditate, walk around the block a few hundred times, talk with your Higher Power, turn it over.

However you decide to handle it, work it through, and don't let it sit inside of you.

Choosing to Confront the Person

You show you care about a relationship when you take responsibility for your feelings and don't use them to attack the other person. A good way to state your case is to say

- what you understand about the situation. That is, *if* you understand the situation after considering all the angles.
- how you feel now, starting sentences with "I" not "You." For example, saying "*I* am really angry with you for . . ." and "*I* get very frustrated when you . . ." shows that you own your feelings and is better than "*You* make me angry when . . ." and "*You* frustrate me when . . ."
- why you're angry. Don't explain it, only let them know what needs of yours weren't met.

I might say to Mike, "Mike, I know you've been really busy lately, but I'm really upset that you're late picking me up. I think you're being inconsiderate when you treat me as if my time isn't important — it is!"

Sometimes — when a person does rude things to you over and over or when you've both let your feelings build up — it takes a heated argument to clear the air. (This is not recommended if you have a history of reacting violently or abusively.) Then, when you cool down, you'll need to go back to sort out what happened and make amends if necessary. If you let people know what you're feeling right away, though, your anger doesn't have to build into resentment or hatred.

You may be thinking, *This all sounds good on paper, but I doubt it works in real life.* Give it a few tries, you might be surprised.

One Last Thing About Anger

How people respond to your confrontation will make a difference in how your relationship with them continues. Hopefully, they will not be defensive, listen openly, and apologize or at least show concern. But you're not in charge of their response. You're only in charge of your feelings and how you express them. Remember, no matter how people respond to you, you can continue to trust how you feel and let people know how you feel.

One last thing about anger: in the end, unresolved anger only hurts you, not the person you're angry at. While you sit in your room for two hours steaming about something your parents said or did (plotting revenge no doubt), they are probably going about their day unaffected by your grudge. So don't hang on to your anger — deal with it, then let it go.

The Big Book says, "If we were to live, we had to be free of anger." Anger is probably one of the hardest feelings to face. If we learn to work through our anger and resentments, understanding and getting through our other painful emotions seem easier.

Hurt

Anger and hurt often go hand in hand. If you are angry, chances are that someone hurt your feelings. Don't be afraid to say, "That hurt my feelings!" when your feelings are hurt. (Pretty basic, huh?) Until you listen to your feelings, you may not even realize when your feelings are hurt. Sometimes our pride gets in the way and we think we'll become too vulnerable by sharing our hurt and pain. More often than not, though, people will respect us for our honesty and sincerity.

We don't have to be alone in our pain. We can talk about it with our sponsor, friends in AA, or another friend or family member we trust.

Jealousy

When we are jealous of someone, we are saying to ourselves, *I can't feel good about myself or be a good person unless I am like this person or have what he or she has.*

We all feel jealous at times, but we can deal with our jealousy in a constructive way. When we feel jealous, we can

- identify what we are jealous about, decide if it's something we truly want, and, if so, set a goal to learn it, buy it, or build that trait into our personality.
- use the occasion to feel good about our own special qualities and remember that each of us is different and no one is better than anyone else.

. . . feel good about your own special qualities . . .

Tim:

> "One day, I was talking to this friend of mine and looking at some paintings she had done. I've always wished I was creative, but I even have trouble drawing stick men, so I said, 'Kathy, you are such a good artist. I wish I was creative like you are.'

> "Then she said, 'But Tim, you have many of your own special talents.' I've never forgotten that. It reminds me to appreciate myself."

Self-Pity — Feeling Sorry For Yourself

What a horrible feeling this is and yet we often seem to enjoy it. Most of us hate to admit it when we're in a pity bag. It seems so self-centered and selfish.

Jessie:

> "I've finally come to the point where I think it's okay to feel sorry for myself sometimes. If I'm feeling this way, I'll usually try to take a night off to pamper myself, you know, take a hot bath and that kind of thing. I'll say to myself up front, *I'm going to feel bad for myself for the entire night.* Well, it never lasts. By the time the night is over, I usually feel ready to take on the world.

> "Sometimes I'll be feeling sorry for myself, like on the bus or something, and then I'll see someone who is worse off than I am and it just snaps me out of it and I remember to count my blessings. It's like my Higher Power is watching over me and saying, 'Hey, shape up.'"

Fear, Worry, Anxiety

Old Proverb: *Ninety percent of what we worry about, never happens.*
Me: *Yeah, but it's the other ten percent I'm worried about.*

Fear, worry, anxiety, nervousness — all of these feelings are normal. For the first few weeks or months of being straight, we can expect our nerves to be shot as we detoxify from all the poisons we put into our body. But we don't have to let these feelings stop us from trying new things and taking risks. In fact, it's when we're trying something new and aren't sure how it's going to come out that we feel most anxious. Many people who've been in the program awhile say that the better their spiritual program is, the more comfortable they are turning fears, worries, and anxiety over to their Higher Power.

Ashanti:

"For me, it helped to start by taking small risks and overcoming my fear that way. Even if you don't succeed right away, you really succeed just by trying.

"Another thing is that it helps to 'live in today,' you know, prepare the best you can and then quit worrying about it.

"Also, when I'm worrying about something that's totally out of my control, I try to keep in touch with my Higher Power, because I truly believe in my heart that my Higher Power would not let anything come my way that I couldn't handle.

"Sometimes I know my fear is legitimate. Like the other night I got off the bus and I had to walk two blocks home in the dark and I live in a bad neighborhood — sometimes I know that my fear is kind of like a warning device."

Guilt, Shame, and Self-Blame

Believe it or not, guilt has some practical uses. When you feel guilty about something, think of your conscience telling you that you're uncomfortable with your behavior — that what you're doing is not in line with what you believe is right.

If you promise to keep your room clean and to do your part around the house and don't follow through, you'll probably feel guilty. Your guilt is letting you know that your behavior is not in line with the kind of person you said you wanted to be.

If you feel guilty about something, instead of sitting around beating yourself up, *do* something:

- Make amends so you can feel better and quit blaming yourself.
- Change your behavior to reflect your values.
- If you notice a lot of guilt piling up, do another Fourth and Fifth Step.

Shame is different from guilt. Guilt says, "I did a bad thing, I should've cleaned my room." Shame says, "I'm a bad person, I never do the right thing."

Shame encourages the belief, *I am basically bad, defective, unworthy, and inadequate.* This kind of thinking may have come from past abuse, either emotional or physical. When we were very young, we may have been made to believe through what people said to us or how they acted toward us, that we were somehow bad or defective. Eventually, we began to believe that message and gave it to ourselves. Some of our acting out may have been to play the role of the bad kid that we had taken on.

In order to get rid of our shame, we need to slowly, over time, replace the negative beliefs we have about ourselves with positive, self-loving beliefs, such as *I am a good person. I have unique and special gifts. It's okay to make mistakes; everyone does.* And, *it's okay when people disagree with me or act as if they don't like me. I know I'm okay.*

Getting past our shame and really feeling good about who we are is a long and hard process. Shame affects every aspect of our life. We may even need professional counseling to help us through it. But shame doesn't have to consume our entire life. We *can* make changes, One Day at a Time.

Grief, Sadness, and Depression

There's a lot to grieve about when we decide to go straight. No matter how good we may feel about beginning a new, drug-free life we will still have times when we miss our drugs. We grieve the loss of the easy "good feelings" from getting high. Drugs were our best friend. Now, they're gone.

Most of us have probably lost people friends too. Friends who are still using often have no interest in us when we're straight. And we may decide it's too dangerous to keep those old relationships built only on sharing the next high.

Grief and sadness and even periods of depression are natural emotions; there will always be things in life that sadden us. But if we find ourselves depressed most of the time and can't seem to feel good even when things are going fine, we may need extra help.

If you constantly feel tired, uninterested in things that usually interest you, or have self-destructive thoughts regularly, you probably need professional help to get through your depression. Some serious depressions may need to be treated with antidepressant medication. These medications don't get people high and are not addictive. They simply allow a person's natural brain chemistry to achieve balance. In most cases, they only have to be taken temporarily until the person's brain chemistry returns to normal.

Usually, though, by dealing with our feelings (especially our anger), learning to replace self-defeating thinking with positive thinking, and resolving or breaking with our painful pasts, we can heal.

A Final Emotional Plea

All of the emotions I've talked about can be very hard to deal with, but no painful feeling is permanent. Remember:

- Don't deny your feelings.
- Talk about your feelings.
- Use your Higher Power.
- Go to Twelve Step meetings regularly.
- Be thankful you can feel. There was probably a time you couldn't.
- If your bad feelings are extreme, seem out of control, or persist for a long time, get some professional counseling or join a self-help group.

Keep in mind, too, that the anger or hurt other people feel is very real to them, even if it doesn't make sense to you. Try to be open-minded. If you hurt someone, apologize. Sometimes people just want to know you care. Make amends if necessary.

What Do Feelings Have To Do with Relationships?

If someone confronts you with how he or she feels, try not to be defensive.

Each of us has talents, interests, and feelings that help to make up our personality. Some of our personality traits stay pretty much the same, but we also change with time and new challenges. We will uncover talents we didn't know we had, develop new interests, and learn to recognize and express our feelings. This doesn't happen in isolation, but as the result of being with other people — each with their own unique talents, interests, and feelings. Our feelings — about ourselves and other people — are what guide us in our relationships as we set boundaries and make friends.

The main difference between dealing with our feelings when we're straight and when we were using is this: When we were controlled by our addiction, we mostly *reacted* to people and situations, and felt out of control. In recovery, we can *act* from inside ourselves because we're learning to know and trust who we are.

You have a wonderful opportunity. You have choices now in determining who you want to be. Ask yourself, *What kind of person do I want to be? Do I want to cool my hot temper? Do I need to become a better listener? More talkative?*

As you ask yourself these kinds of questions and decide what kind of person you want to be, you'll discover new things about yourself, and you'll be able to try out new "possible selves" with friends, parents, teachers, and at AA or NA meetings.

Slowly, you'll find that you are acting more and more from your own beliefs instead of reacting to the people and situations around you. And believe me, it feels great!

Shawn:

"Sometimes I know I don't deal with things the way I should. Like with my folks — they are just so stuck in their way of thinking. A lot of the time when I'm pissed off at them, I don't even bother talking to them because they're just going to do it their way anyway.

"Sometimes I just don't care. As long as I stay straight, that's all that matters. Things will be better once I'm not living under *their* roof."

Michelle:

"With relationships, I'm more assertive, you know, I help make decisions and also I'm not the only one working for the relationship. It's not just me, myself, and I, you know.

"With my old boyfriend, when it was near the end of our relationship, it was just me. I called him; I asked him to do things; I asked him to come over; I told him when I was coming over — things like that. You know, he got kind of lazy. He never called me back because he knew I'd call. It was 99 percent me and 1 percent him. It wasn't much of a relationship because I was reaching out and he wasn't.

"Another thing is, I'm not always angry at Jon, my new boyfriend. Sometimes I'll get a little irritated just because he's obnoxious and sometimes embarrassing, but I'm not always angry. I've learned that that's Jon. I don't have to be embarrassed for Jon. Just because I'm sitting by him or I'm his girlfriend doesn't mean I have to be embarrassed for him. I've learned that."

Jon:

"It's just incredible how I get along with my mom, except with like appreciation and stuff like that. Just telling her how I feel, that's really hard. I have no idea why.

"I think I'm more honest with her though. My relationship with her before was built on lies. After treatment, it was really a shock because I could tell her where I was going. It doesn't sound like much, but it was something. The honesty makes a real big difference and, I think, really cuts down the resentment."

Before, my relationship with my mom was built on lies.

Sheila:

"I've been trying to get my mom to realize that I need some of her time, you know. I need her to take time away from going out on dates or going to work. I mean, I realize that she works a lot, but . . .

"I told her the other day — I got really upset — and I said, 'Mom, can you come here? I need to talk to you.' Then I said, 'You're going out *again*? I'm not telling you to just drop everything and come running to me, but I do need *some* of your time. I do need for you to take time out.'

"When I was using I would have just got mad and told her she didn't care and that she didn't love me."

Wayne:

"Since I went through treatment, my brother and I get along so good it's unreal. We still fight, but it's different. Like the other day, he took one of my favorite tapes without asking me. When he got home, I told him how *I* felt. I said, 'Andy, I'm really upset about what you did. It's like I'm invisible and like you could care less if I wanted to listen to that tape or not.' He was mad at first, but I just kept saying how *I* felt. What could he say? I felt how I felt."

Tammy:

"I've had a lot of problems trusting both females and males, but I've found several friends. I think I have better perception now. Before, I didn't open my eyes to look at their true character, you know, I never looked any further than the drugs they had or the people they knew. Now I go for deeper things like 'How well do we relate in our interests?' and 'How well do we relate in our beliefs?'"

Joe:

"My mom and I get along really good. Before, I didn't listen to her. I defied her all the time, you know. She kept on threatening to send me to a group home, but I kept on defying her. Now I get along really good with her. When I was using, I didn't give a shit about anything."

Erin:

"When I was using, I was afraid of my dad. I liked him, but I was afraid he might find me out, afraid he might judge me, afraid that he'd look down on me because I was having sex and I was too young.

"Another thing about my dad is that I always feel like I'm doing things wrong when I'm around him. I'm trying to get over that and work on it, but I haven't really talked to him about it. That's one thing I should do, but I don't know if it's him or me. I feel that he expects me to do too much, and I get down on myself when I don't do it. It hurts, but it doesn't hurt me enough to make me want to go back to using. If I used, it wouldn't make it any better. It wouldn't change it . . . it'd make it worse because I'd close up again."

Josh:

"I used to get to do anything I wanted, so when I came home from treatment it was pretty tough having a curfew and things like that. I really hate it sometimes, but at least I feel like my stepdad and mom are flexible. You know, if I sit down and present my reasoning in an adult way, they're more open. It helps to talk to my mom alone, too, and let her talk to my stepdad."

Sierra:

"My sister got me the most angry because she brought beer in the house and I felt she didn't have no respect for me. I just hate it, knowing that she's got that little respect for me, you know, bringing people over to the house that are so high that they can't even talk.

"Last night she drove home and was so high when she walked in the door, her eyes were so glossy, that it looked like she couldn't even see straight, let alone talk. Then she wanted me to get up and fix her a bowl of cereal. I said no. I said, 'If you can drive home and go out all hours of the night and want something to eat at three in the morning, you can fix it yourself.'

"I just get so angry with her I want to take her head off. Last night I just said, 'I give up. I can't take it no more.' She has no respect for me. I've been giving and giving and giving and I'm not receiving a thing. None of the messages I've been giving are getting through to her. I've just had it. I'll take care of myself. I'm not going to let her get in the way of what I need to do for myself."

Tanya:

"Before, I would say, 'Go to my dad's? What fun is that? What am I going to talk about with my dad? When he asks me what I did this weekend, am I supposed to say, 'Well dad, I went to a party and got real high. I couldn't walk, and Lord knows how I got home?'

"Before, when he'd ask me over for dinner or something, it was 'No, sorry dad, I can't. I made plans already.'

"Now I make time for him. It means a lot to him. He gets so excited to see me and that makes me feel good."

Chad:

"I talk with my mom now, like about everyday stuff even. When I was using it was straight to my room and shut off from the world. Now I talk to my mom."

Breaking the Ties

If you are in an unhealthy or abusive relationship and it's clear the other person won't change, you need to get out. Staying sober and working your program means giving yourself the chance to grow and change. You can't take advantage of those opportunities if you're in an abusive relationship. You can make the choices now that will give you the best life has to offer.

Ask yourself these questions:

- Am I getting anything out of this relationship or is it one-sided?
- Am I free to be who I am and become what I want to become?
- Do I feel supported in my need to grow and change?
- Does the relationship push me into acting out the same old role all the time?
- Is the other person physically, verbally, or emotionally abusive or otherwise trying to control me?
- Do I feel good about myself with this person?
- Am I, for the most part, happy when we're together?

Breaking the ties of an unhealthy relationship can be scary. Often, we're afraid of hurting the other person. But if we have become so unhappy that we need out, it's likely that the relationship is not the best thing for the other person either. It's better to end it now rather than risk being hurt much worse later.

Ideally, you will be able to sit down with the person and explain how you feel. But this is not always possible. There are times when it's best to make a clean break, which means stopping all contact immediately.

If the person is physically abusive, you need to get away — right now! You might want to check into services your community offers for helping people leave an abusive relationship. Even if you don't need a place to stay, shelters for victims of battering may be able to give you some good information about your rights and how to protect yourself.

Dealing with Authority, *Or* "What Do You Mean I Can't Do That?"

If certain authority figures grated on your nerves when you were using, you aren't necessarily going to be buddy-buddy now that you're straight. It's not like two tablespoons of AA, a half cup of a Higher Power, four quarts of personal inventory and voila! Instant teacher's pet. (You probably wouldn't want that anyway.)

What Do I Mean
By Authority Figures?

- If you're living at home, you are probably going to have some restrictions put on you by your parents.
- If you live in a group home or halfway house, no doubt there are rules and regulations to follow and somebody to enforce them.
- If you're in or going back to school, you'll be dealing with teachers, principals, guidance counselors, and coaches.
- Unless you own your own business, you'll have to work for someone else if you want money, which means they have authority.
- And then there are police, parole officers, landlords, therapists, sponsors (sometime authority figures), and anyone who legally or by more experience or knowledge than you has been given some power over you.

Toni:

> "I have this one teacher that I just hate. The whole school hates him. He gets off on pushing people around. He just thinks he's 'Joe Cool' or something.
>
> "Anyway, when I was using I used to get into it with him all the time, so I had to think about how I was going to handle him when I got back in school.
>
> "So the first time he started layin' into me, I just said, 'Hey, I don't want to get into it with you.' I was really calm and everything. I had to say it twice, but he backed off. It was unreal."

Tyler:

> "I used to deal with authority figures by telling them what they wanted to hear. I'd just agree with everything they said, listen to their lectures, and then go out and do what I wanted to.

171

"Now I say when I don't agree and I argue my point. If I'm not going to do it, then I say I'm not going to do it. Sometimes I'll agree to do it, even if I don't want to, but then I'll say 'I'll do it, but I'm not okay with this and I don't think it's fair.'"

Matt:

"I guess I know now that most of these people are just doing their jobs. I may not like it, but it's just their jobs."

You Mean These Are People?

Yes, believe it or not, authority figures are people just like you and me. It may be a struggle to remember this, but they are human and have lives, fears, and flaws just like everyone else.

We can learn something from almost everybody we meet. Everybody has a bit of knowledge from which we could benefit, and most important, that may teach us something about ourselves.

A good parent, teacher, or sponsor will help us unlock our own wisdom and be the best person we can be.

Our part in all of this is becoming open to what others can give us.

We can learn to recognize when someone can help us become who we want to be. "Authority figures" can become people *we* give the authority to help and guide us. Everyone, even authority figures, needs help, guidance, discipline, and structure in his or her life.

Even "bad" parents, teachers, or sponsors teach us something about ourselves. Maybe we learn from our relationships with them how to confront situations rather than run; how to talk calmly rather than shout; and how to know when to quit and get out of a situation. We don't always have to be thankful for the bad stuff in our life. It may come down to just knowing that we can grow and achieve *in spite* of some people who haven't been positive role models.

Getting along with anyone can be trying, but when a person has some authority over you, getting along can seem impossible!

There are so many different kinds of authority relationships that it's hard to apply the same rules to all situations, but let's try a few basics.

1. *Know where you're at.* When you started using, you arrested your emotional development. If you started using at eleven, it's quite possible that you're still around eleven years old emotionally, even if you're eighteen now. If you feel as if you're being treated like a child, maybe that's the way you've been acting. No blame or shame here, this is just a part of the illness of chemical dependency. It maybe easier to understand that part of you may need to be taken care of and part of you wants to be treated as an adult. This can be awfully confusing for parents, teachers, and other authority figures.

2. *Know where they're at.* Sometimes it's hard to approach a parent because we see him or her as nosy, boring, bossy, and unfair — as parents, not people. A teacher may appear to us as a cardboard figure with no feelings whose only purpose is to bore us with useless facts and humiliate us with meaningless tests. Maybe we cast our supervisor as a power hungry slave driver, or cops as bullies — the list goes on. What we may forget is that apart from the role we give them, each of these people has a life with hopes and hassles a lot like the ones we have.

   You probably aren't going to start filling your social schedule with time for your teachers, parents, or supervisors, but being willing to see authority figures as human can make a difference. If your parents ask you where you've been, maybe they're really interested in you. And it may be interesting to find out how they are feeling, how things are at work, what they thought of a movie.

3. *Be honest.* When you acknowledge where you are at and that authority figures are human, it's easier to be honest with the way you're really feeling. Even if you disagree with an authority figure and are angry

because you feel a rule or expectation is unfair, the relationship is easier to handle if you see authority figures as human and not as a symbol of power.

How to Rebel — This Is Where You Get to Be Creative

There are times when rules or expectations are unfair and we need to take care of ourselves and be assertive. Healthy rebellion is how we change things, break from dependence on our family, and discover who we are. How we rebel makes all the difference — our tone of voice, posture, and facial expression may say more than our words.

If I scream my grievances in my boss's face, I'm more likely to get fired than heard. But if I sit down with him or her and calmly discuss the situation, I'm more likely to get heard than fired.

Here's a five point plan formulated from my decades and decades of experience. (Okay, so it's only months and months — decades just sounded more authoritative.)

1. *Present your case.* Talk to the person, either by yourself or with another person if appropriate, in a calm respectful manner, and present just the facts. As much as possible, try to talk in sentences that begin "I . . . ," not "You . . . ," and deal with the situation, not his or her personality. If you need to say something personal, let him or her know your feelings, don't blame.

2. *Give solutions.* Don't lay the problem in the other person's lap so you can criticize his or her solutions. Offer some of your own solutions that meet your needs and that acknowledge the other person's concerns.

3. *Be consistent and persistent.* If it is an ongoing problem, be willing to try different things until it's solved. Stay in there and show you care, and not just about getting your way but about coming up with a solution that's best for all concerned.

175

4. *Know your next move.* How big of a deal is this to you? When you've followed all the rules and tried your best with little or no results, what will you do next? Ask yourself, *Is this worth hassling with or should I just drop it?*

5. *Toss points one through four if you have to.* The first four points of this plan are not etched in stone — they won't magically get you what you need every time. Maybe being nice about the situation didn't work. Maybe you're fed up and want something done now. Do what you have to do then, but ask yourself two questions: (1) *Am I doing this to right a wrong, to serve an important cause, or to satisfy my need to win a power struggle?* and (2) *What are the consequences of my actions?*

If your sobriety is in anyway threatened, you have your priorities out of order and may need to just drop it.

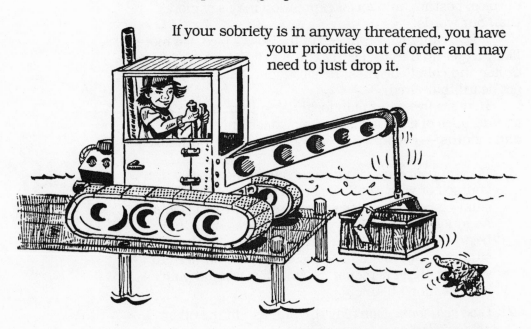

Is this worth hassling with or should I just drop it?

Ashanti:

"Just about a month ago, I wanted to stay out until two o'clock, but my folks always want me in by midnight, so I asked them about it.

"There was this party I wanted to go to. It was a straight party and they were going to have a band, which almost never happens. Everyone I talked to was going to stay that late, so I wanted to too.

"I asked my parents and they said no. I got so mad, I just lost it and we got into this huge fight, with me losing, of course.

"The next day I felt bad about what happened and I sat down and talked with them calmly to say I was sorry. I told them why it was so important to me and how I felt and they said I could go to the party.

"I'm sure they said I could go because of the way I handled it, because I didn't say anything that I hadn't already said when we were fighting. I think it was just the way I said it that worked."

Chuck:

"I got pulled over the other day and got a ticket for speeding — going forty in a thirty-five. Do you believe it? I was so pissed. This cop must have been having a slow day to give me a ticket for that! I wanted to lip off so bad. I don't know why I didn't. I guess I just figured that it would only make things worse."

Brandon:

"In biology, they wanted us to dissect a cat and I didn't want to do it, so I asked my teacher for a different project. I just don't think it's right to use animals that way. I've read about it and it reinforces the belief that animals are 'things' to use as we please.

"I talked to the teacher and the principal and offered to do a 'fake dissection' with this computer program that they have now. They said no way and that if I didn't do the cat dissection, I'd fail the whole class.

"I told them to fail me. I don't care if I don't graduate — I'm not doing it and they can't make me. It's the principle of the thing."

Julaine:

"I hate my job. I don't get along with anyone there except maybe one or two people. The people there are so sick — always cutting each other down and stuff.

"Sometimes I get so mad at them that I want to slash their tires! I'm serious. I think of stuff like that.

"I went to an NA meeting the other night and this woman there said maybe I should quit my job. She said it sounded like it wasn't a very healthy environment.

"I had thought about quitting before, but I kept thinking the problem was me, like I should be more tolerant or something. It was good to hear someone else's ideas.

"I'm looking for a new job now. I'm going to quit as soon as I find one."

Tammy:

"I'm a lot more sympathetic toward police now, because they have a hell of a job and I wouldn't want it.

"At work, I feel that some people abuse their power, but there's not a lot I can do about it except talk to them or talk to their higher up. I don't want to lose my job, so a lot of times I just kind of bite down on my anger and say 'fine,' then I vent it when I get out of the place.

"When it comes to politics, I'm very firm in my beliefs. You could even say 'opinionated.' And if there is an authority figure, you know, a politician or whoever going against what I believe, I will raise one hell of a protest."

Jon:

"I wasn't the kind of kid who would confront the teacher face-to-face. I would just act cool. My attitude toward them wasn't really that bad. I just had a hard time realizing that 'Okay, this is the way it is,' you know, 'I'm in school now and I'm going to have to follow these rules.'"

Sierra:

"I've never been one for authority. I don't know what it was about not wanting to do what they said, it's just that I felt like it was something I *had* to do. I wasn't going to do something just because they said I *had* to.

"Now, if I start screwin' off, the teachers think I'm going to react the way I did last year when I was using. Then, there goes my grades, there goes the goals I have for school, there goes everything. I guess that's one thing that pulls me up a lot of the time. I want to meet my goals."

Karen:

"I think authority bothers me more now because I'm more aware of what they're doing. When I'm rebellious or when I go against something they say, it's because I have a reason to. It's not just empty rebellion, but rebellion because I disagree with something that they're doing and I want to change it.

"Things that help . . . I was on the school newspaper for a while and it helped coming up with good stories to dig up dirt and get ideas out. I'm also in Amnesty International and I try and do what I can through that. It's hard to stand up for what you believe in, because so many times you get knocked down.

"I don't have a lot of problem with authority because I'm so responsible and I don't want to get in trouble and there's something deep down in me that doesn't want to make waves, but at the same point I know there are times when I should."

Chad:

"I just do what I'm supposed to do because of the good feelings I get from it. You know, if my mom asks me to do the dishes or something, I just do it rather than bitch about it because I feel good afterwards."

Maria:

"The thing that's hard for me about authority is that when I feel like I'm helpless and that someone is 'making' me do something, that's when I want to get high the most.

"I need to make sure that the things I'm doing in my life I'm doing because I *want* to. When I want to get high, I need to go to a meeting and get in touch with the fact that I *want* to stay straight."

180

Is It All Worth It?

The answer is yes! Recovering is a reprieve from the crippling isolation of addiction. It means being welcomed back to the human race. It means enjoying who we are again, which frees us to enjoy others for who they are.

Most of us find that the longer we're straight, the more rewarding our relationships with other people become. As we change, our relationships will change. With sobriety, we can reach out to others to find what we were looking for all the while we were using — the peace of belonging.

Unplanning Your Slips, *Or* How to Hang On To The Wagon

Slips Can't Be Taken Lightly

Okay, everybody slips, right? You can walk into nearly any young people's Narcotics Anonymous or Alcoholics Anonymous meeting, and you'll meet a number of people who have had one or more slips. Some of them have been with the program for years. So what's the big deal?

You may meet someone like Tom, who has been going to AA for about a year, but every three months, just before he gets a medallion, he'll use. Whether it's a one night drunk or a long binge, it's always back to AA to start over.

Or maybe you know someone like Diane. She was straight for eight months before she started using again. Her relapse lasted six weeks. Now, after being sober for another seven months, she says, "It seems like everyone slips at least once. It's almost like you expect it. I don't mean to make light of it or anything, but I think a lot of young people figure that the program will always be here, so they can always come back."

Slips do seem to be taken lightly. Even the very nature of the word slip, brings to mind someone saying, "Oops, I made a boo-boo."

Well, slips should be taken very seriously.

On the page dated October 9th in the meditation book, *Day by Day*, this is what is said about slips:

> *A common rationalization about not making the program goes like this: "Harry over there*

*slipped 10 times before he made it, so what
if I slip a few times?"*

*What is overlooked is the last time Jack
slipped — he slipped into a coffin; the last
time Bob slipped — his baby son burned to
death in a crib because of his negligence; the
last time Ann slipped — she got strychnine
poisoning and is blind . . .*

*We're not playing games here — this is a
matter of life and death. Have I stopped
slipping?*

*Lord, let me know that it is not only my life,
but the lives of others that I endanger by
playing loaded games.*[1]

Many of us know at least one person who has suffered a tragedy because of going back to using. Take
Johnny. He was eighteen and had been straight for two
and a half years when he started using again. It seemed
totally harmless at first, but it turned into a month-long
spree that did a lot of damage. It ended with the robbery
of a liquor store, and Johnny spending over a year in jail.

Roxanne relapsed with six months' sobriety when
she was twenty years old. It lasted only one night, but
that was long enough for her to sleep with a stranger
and contract herpes. She'll live with that slip the rest
of her life.

As harsh as these stories sound, they could have
been worse. Roxanne could have contracted AIDS and
lost her life. Johnny could have killed someone during
the robbery.

It's important to remember how serious a slip is;
however, in order to survive a slip, you'd need some
practical ways to get your recovery back on track, not
a lecture. So let's start from the beginning. . . .

---

[1] *Day by Day* (Center City, Minn.: Hazelden Educational
Materials, 1974).

The Morning After

To begin with, we don't have to relapse. At some level, those who relapse plan it. By looking at how relapse happens, we can "unplan" it and devise a method for achieving ongoing sobriety. A life of total abstinence is working, One Day at a Time, for millions of us in Twelve Step programs.

Many people do relapse, though. So imagine you've sabotaged your recovery and had a slip and it's the next day. What would you need to know to go on from there?

What you decide to do the morning after a relapse can be crucial. Chances are, you're going to wake up feeling very badly about your behavior, or you'll have no memory of your behavior at all. Whether you're hung over or not, your thinking will probably be foggy. You may not even be sober yet.

Whatever your state, the first and most important thing you can do is make a commitment to stay straight for the next twenty-four hours, and the surest way to do that is to admit what you did.

It's unlikely you're going to want to tell *anybody* what happened, but keeping it to yourself is the worst thing you can do. You can start by just admitting it fully to yourself, and then asking your Higher Power for help.

Now is the time to take another look at the first three Steps.

Step One:

We admitted we were powerless over alcohol (or "our addiction") — that our lives had become unmanageable.

The fact that we can relapse in the face of all we've learned about chemical dependency is proof of our powerlessness. How unmanageable are things right now?

Step Two:

Came to believe that a Power greater than ourselves could restore us to sanity.

We learned where the strength to stay straight came from — our Higher Power. By relapsing, we relearn the insanity of choosing to use.

Step Three:

Made a decision to turn our will and our lives over to the care of God *as we understood Him.*

Turning it over is an ongoing part of recovery. We may pretend we're all alone at times like this, but our Higher Power never left.

We won't spend pages and pages talking about the first three Steps. Just this: think about what kind of a role your Higher Power has played in your life lately.

Eric:

"Since I've been sober, I catch myself always talking about how I'm in control of things now. That's partially true, but what's really crazy is that I find that I'm at my healthiest and I feel the best about my life when I'm not taking control. What I mean is, when I get in touch with my powerlessness and truly turn issues over to my Higher Power, things seem to go smoother. I'm more at peace. It's all about trust, you know, having faith that I will be okay. Believe me, it's much less stressful!"

Talking to Parents About a Slip

Your next step, if your parents aren't using themselves and you've got a pretty good relationships with them, might be to go and tell them about the slip. Don't be afraid to level with them. You don't have to promise that it will never happen again; just let them know that you had a slip, how bad you're really feeling, and that you need to talk to someone about it.

189

Calling a Friend or Sponsor — The Day After

If you're active in NA or AA, call one of your program friends. It's very important to talk to a straight friend during this first twenty-four hours. If you have a sponsor, make him or her your first choice. If not, find a good listener, someone who won't judge you. It's much easier to tell someone the day after it happens than six weeks later.

Going to a Meeting — The Day After

At the very least, sometime during this first twenty-four hours after your slip, go to an AA or NA meeting. Even if it's not your regular meeting, even if you don't talk. Just go!

Do whatever you have to do to stay out of situations where you might use. Staying away from temptation and talking to people you trust will give you an opportunity to *evaluate* your relapse.

Evaluating the Slip

Some of you may be thinking, *Geez, all I do is have a few beers and then I have to pick my brain apart?* Not really. Whatever you do is your decision, but the sooner you talk to someone and evaluate your relapse, the better your chances for having a real choice the next time you're in a situation where relapse is a risk.

When you talk about your slip, go over these questions:

- How did it happen?
- What did you like about the slip?
- What didn't you like about the slip?
- What do you like about being straight?
- Do you like yourself better when you're using or when you're straight?

190

How Did It Happen?

The idea here is not to come up with a bunch of excuses, but to see if there was a pattern of behavior that led up to your relapse. If you can see a pattern of behavior, it will help you prevent a relapse in the future.

While the list of behaviors that can bring on a slip is endless, chances are you were into some form of *stinkin' thinkin'*.

Stinkin' thinkin' refers to all the little games our mind can play with us — all the B.S. that we can come up with to justify taking the first drink or hit.

. . . talk to someone and evaluate your relapse.

Cindy:

"I was out with a group of old friends that I hadn't seen in awhile. We went out for pizza and were just talking about old times and stuff, and I was having a great time. They were all drinking wine and exotic drinks, and I was drinking pop. I don't know what I was thinking, but they kept talking about how good this wine was and how good that drink was, and they were all tasting each other's drinks.

"Finally I asked to taste a sip of wine. *Just one sip!* What harm could that do, right? I mean, I figured I just wanted to taste it; I wasn't drinking it because I wanted to get loaded or anything. It's really amazing because, at the time, I really didn't see the harm. Well, it didn't stop with one sip. I had another and pretty soon I tried a drink. It was a horrible night. I was in relapse off and on for about three months.

"Now I'm really on my guard when I start thinking insane thoughts like I can just have a taste and not have to get high. I talk about my thoughts at meetings. I realize now that I can work through my doubts and my negative head trips without using. Not even a sip."

Nicolas:

"I think I had my slip because I started to have all these resentments inside of me about everything. It started with feeling angry at my brother because he was still using. I was evaluating him and thinking he needed to be straight. I really resented the fact that he didn't care that he was still using. He didn't see that he had a problem.

"Then I started to resent being chemically dependent. All my resentments just snowballed and then I started wondering if I really was alcoholic. Well, next thing I knew, I was getting high. It's hard to say that my slip was caused by one thing. I mean, I think it was a combination of things that led up to my slip, but I do know that if you allow the negative crap to build, it's going to fall right on top of you."

Now you need to ask yourself these questions:

- Have I cut down on meetings, or stopped going altogether?
- Have I quit hanging around with sober people?
- Do I have a sponsor? Do I *call* my sponsor?
- Have I been working the program One Day at a Time?
- Have I been sharing the program?

When Susan, a seventeen-year-old with one year of sobriety, had her slip, she didn't even realize that her behavior had changed. Although she had attended three meetings a week, she cut back to one, and she started spending more time with the people from work who used.

192

Susan:

"I knew other people in AA who only went to one meeting a week and who didn't hang around with AA people very much. They seemed to be doing okay, so I didn't see the harm. I just wasn't getting it through my head that what someone else does isn't necessarily what's good for me.

"I *need* three meetings a week and I feel great about that. I keep in touch with healthy people. It keeps me healthy. Now I keep in touch with what works for me."

Dan:

"My girlfriend and I usually communicate pretty well, you know, we make an effort to share our appreciation and resentments. Well, just before my slip, I realize now that I was constantly picking fights with her. You know, criticizing her and being really self-righteous. I used our fights as an excuse. I would give myself the old "poor me" treatment and tell her that she just didn't know what it was like for me. And then, of course, I had a *reason* to drink. Now, when I catch myself picking fights, I ask myself, *Why do I want an excuse to use?* And I change my behavior."

What Did You Like About the Slip?

Your first reaction to this question may be, "What?! You want me to talk about what I *liked* about using?"

It may sound crazy, but finding out what appealed to you about getting drunk or stoned may help you understand why being sober can be hard.

Rick:

"The morning after my slip, I was extremely embarrassed about a lot of the things I had done the night before. What was weird though, is that when I was drunk that night, it was the first time in six months I had really let myself go, you know — just acted how I wanted to.

"When I'm straight, I get into trying to be perfect. I concentrate so much on taking my inventory and always saying the right thing that I forget to have fun. I'm learning that I can just loosen up, not take myself so seriously and still lead a sober life.

"When I think about what I like about using, it's really easy for me to think only of the good times and not the bad. Usually, my memories are pretty distorted. I used to think that I was so funny and fun to be around, you know, a *fun drunk,* but it's just not true. In reality, I was loud and obnoxious. I have to be real honest with myself when thinking about my using days and see myself for what I was."

Like Rick, we often only remember the *good times* of being high and block out what really was going on — the real damage we did to ourselves and others. We realize we can find only in sobriety the genuine relaxed self-acceptance, closeness with others, and positive feelings our disease falsely promised that we'd get from alcohol and other drugs.

What Didn't You Like About the Slip?

Although this question may seem obvious, if you don't make a point to think about it, it's very easy to skim over.

Think through your using behavior and try to remember specifically what you didn't like. This can range from having said something stupid or having slept with someone you didn't care for to not liking how the drugs made your body feel. Be careful not to blame your behavior on someone or something else. For example, it's not the police officer's fault that you got a DWI, it's yours. Take responsibility for your behavior.

Christine:

"When I don't take responsibility for my behavior, I'm saying 'It's not my fault if I get stoned.' I blame everything and everybody around me for how I act. But when I fix the blame everywhere but where it belongs, I eliminate all my choices, you know. Then *I'm* out of control, and then I'm back to using."

While asking yourself what you didn't like about how you acted when you slipped, also ask yourself if you would have handled things differently had you been straight at the time. You're a lot less likely to go against your values and lie, hurt, or endanger yourself and other people, or jump into bed with somebody you don't know (and wouldn't want to know), if you're straight.

Kevin:

"I was at an outdoor party when I slipped. There was a guy there who was acting like he thought he was really cool. I was pretty loaded and well, to make a long story short, he started shooting off his

196

mouth and I started shooting off my mouth, and we really got into it.

"He ended up beatin' the crap out of me. It was really a drag. The next morning I just thought, *What a stupid way to deal with things.* It just wasn't worth getting worked up about. I know if I hadn't been using, I would've just ignored the guy and probably laughed it off."

Sherri:

"The morning after my slip, I got a call from a friend, and she started talking about the parked car I hit the night before when I was driving her home. I had absolutely no memory of hitting anything. I had to go out to the driveway and look at my car before I believed her. When I saw the dent on my car, I knew it was true. I am so against drinking and driving — and here I had just done that very thing. All I could think about the next day was, *What if it had been a little kid I had run over? Would I have even remembered?*"

What Do You Like About Being Straight?

The answers to this question can run from "No hangovers" to "A deeper awareness of life and energy around me." Ask yourself the following questions about your life when you're straight.

- Do you feel more confident?
- Do you have more self-respect?
- Do you have the respect of others?
- Is your life starting to have some direction?
- Are you starting to learn what a positive attitude really is?
- Are you more responsible?
- Do you feel you have more choices?
- Are you trusted by others?
- Are you more at peace?
- Aren't you just happy you don't get into trouble every other day?

What do *you* like about being straight?

Some people will have a list of 110 things and some people, like eighteen-year-old Heidi, will have just one.

Heidi:

"When I was using, I tried to keep from feeling anything, but no matter what I did, the shame was still there. Now that I'm straight, every aspect of my life is better, because I know that I can deal with it. That's it."

Do You Like Yourself Better When You're Using or When You're Straight?

By now, you've probably talked with a friend and evaluated the slip pretty thoroughly (and probably run up quite a tab, if you're at a restaurant). It's now time to ask yourself, *Do I like myself better when I'm using or when I'm straight?*

It's crucial to realize that nobody *has* to be straight. After all the soul-searching and evaluating, you may decide to continue using. Leading a clean and sober life is a *choice*, not a prison term!

If you decide to continue using, you may encounter problems similar to those mentioned in the October 9th reading from *Day by Day*. (See pages 184-185.)

Hopefully, after answering some of the questions in this chapter, you'll decide that you've gone through enough because of your using, and you want to be straight today.

Hopefully, you'll decide that you like yourself better when you're straight, that the best way to reach your goals is through clean, sober living. If so, *welcome back!*

A Plan of Action

Well, now that you've made it through another twenty-four hours of not using, where do you go from here?

Doing the self-evaluation should give you a good idea of what you need to do (or not do). Everybody's program is different, but here are some basics that will get you started:

- *Relearn the Twelve Steps and what they mean to you.* Many times you'll hear people talking about "working" the Steps, and perhaps that's a little confusing. It may help if you think of your program as a lifestyle rather than work. Be honest with yourself, think about the Steps daily, apply the principles of AA in your contact with other people, and evaluate your progress. Just Keep it Simple and allow this way of thinking to become a natural part of you.

199

- *Make a commitment daily to stay straight for twenty-four hours.* Sometimes you have to take it minute by minute instead of day by day. Don't forget the Serenity Prayer:

  > God grant me the serenity
  > To accept the things I cannot change,
  > The courage to change the things I can,
  > And the wisdom to know the difference.

- *Keep in touch with your Higher Power.* It's a great feeling to know that you are not alone. You don't have to "do it all" and take total control. You will benefit over and over from the trust and faith you put into your relationship with your Higher Power.
- *Get in the habit of reading daily from AA or NA material and other inspirational writings.* Find a meditation book that feels right, and keep your healthy thinking recharged.
- *Attend at least one, preferably two, AA or NA meetings weekly.* Surround yourself with straight people. You might even try ninety meetings in ninety days — a tried and true formula recommended by the old-timers.

As part of your plan of action, visualize how you'll handle a temptation to use. Close your eyes and picture it as though it's happening. What will you say? What will you do? Feel those proud feelings that you'll feel when you decide to stay straight.

Mike:

"I thought being with my old using friends was going to be pretty tough, but it really wasn't. When someone would ask, 'You want to go get high?' I would say, 'No, thanks anyway.' Once in awhile I get harassed, but not normally. I just leveled with my friends up front and said, 'I'm not dealing with things very good right now and I need to stay straight for a while.' I used to find it hard to believe, but people will respect you for being honest."

As you follow your plan of action, you'll become more and more the person you really want to be.

Today Is a New Day

For those of us who have had a slip, it's natural to have regrets and grieve over having stayed straight so long — only to relapse. While it's important to fully evaluate a slip, and learn from it, that doesn't mean we need to beat ourselves over the head. At some point, we need to put it behind us and just be thankful we're clean and sober *today*.

Most important, we don't have to have a slip to learn all this. By thinking through this process and taking action early, we can catch ourselves and *unplan* a relapse before it happens.

We are all more likely to choose to be straight when we believe we deserve all the wonderful possibilities that sober living, One Day at a Time, can bring. So let's spend the rest of this chapter talking about how we can make some of those possibilities happen. Let's talk about boredom — and its cures.

Bored Straight? *Or,*

Not Another Saturday Night

"What do you people do on Saturday nights?" was my first question at my first AA meeting. I'll never forget the burst of laughter from the group. I was totally puzzled. I wanted to stay straight, but the future looked pretty boring.

Finally, a cute, blond-haired guy spoke up, "I'll tell you what. This Saturday night, Kathleen's having a party at her house. Why don't you come with us and check it out?"

I said, "A *straight* party? What a bizarre concept. All right, why not? I'll go."

"By the way," the blonde guy added, "the best thing about being straight at a party is that you *remember* how much fun you had."

The party was great and it was the beginning of a whole new way of having fun for me — fun without using.

Now you may be thinking, *Yeah, that sounds good, but no one I know holds straight parties, so what am I supposed to do?*

I know it's hard at times to think of something different to do, especially if you're short of cash or without a car. So in this section we'll look at some ideas for having fun the drug-free way. The next time you're sitting around trying to think of a way to entertain yourself, you can just turn to this section for inspiration!

We're not talking miracles here. I mean, when it comes right down to it, it's up to you to get motivated to try different things. I hope to simply give you a few suggestions you may not have thought of before.

Heather:

"Some of the things we consider fun, someone who's using would probably think are totally stupid. When I was using, I probably would have thought they are stupid too. A couple of weeks ago, me and a couple of my straight friends drove about sixty miles to visit my grandma. On the way home, we saw a park, you know, swings and slides and stuff. I know this sounds crazy, but we spent a couple of hours in the park and just played. It was just a blast! I'm sure anyone who saw us thought we were on drugs or something, but it was great because we could just be ourselves and have fun."

Beth:

"Anything you want to do. We bum around, go to concerts, go to plays. Anything."

Vickie:

"Sometimes we'll just hop in a car and take a road trip somewhere. It's great, you can just be spontaneous."

Jim:

"We all get together and play volleyball or softball. Other times, we'll just go B.S. with people, or my girlfriend, Laurie, and I will go see our relatives. We try to be creative with what we do in our spare time, but that's good, so we aren't doing the same thing over and over."

Renee:

"Dance, dance, dance. I love it!"

Justin:

"I like to shoot pool or just play with my dog. It's great when you're straight because with using it was always the same old thing, you know. 'Okay, who's got the weed?' and 'What are we going to do? Well, okay, let's get stoned.' Always the same.

"We've got old granite quarries in town that have filled up with rain water. We go out there when it's hot and go swimming.

"Something I do now that I would've never done when I was using is I mow my grandma's lawn about once a week. Then, I visit with her. At first I thought, *God, this is really a goody-goody thing to do*, but I don't care if it is because I really get a good feeling from it. I mean, I'm no saint — she pays me for doing it — but it's nice to have a good excuse to spend some time with her."

Nancy:

"Brian and I like to go to movies or just have friends or other couples over. Sometimes we'll go to a cabin up north and relax."

Kari:

"I date a lot. I like to date different types of guys. I like to get a bunch of people together and watch videos too.

"Things I do now that I wouldn't be doing if I was still using are buying new clothes and taking care of myself. When I was using, I would let myself go and not spend any money on myself, except for drugs. Now I love buying new clothes."

Cory:

"I like to have straight parties at my house. My folks are really cool about it. They let us have the basement to do what we want, so you know, I invite a few friends over, we crank up the tunes, and invent a few exotic nonalcoholic drinks. It's fun. Oh yeah, and I never have to take anybody's keys away!"

Okay, so you've gotten a few ideas, but let's not stop there. We'll break our ideas down into six categories:

- Places to Go
- The Great Outdoors
- The Great Indoors
- Community Involvement
- Self-Improvement
- By Yourself

Places to Go

Think ahead of ways you can make going where you're going a bit more interesting. For instance, if you're going to visit relatives, maybe bring along with you one of your grandparents or a cousin that you haven't seen for a while. If you're going to an art gallery, stop and pick up a book at the library on some famous artist. The only way things become fun and interesting is when you make them that way.

- *AA or NA Meetings* — Of course, you know this, but it is the number one priority, and not only because of the benefits it has for your sobriety. It's also a great place to meet straight people who you can take with you on all sorts of adventures.

Places to Socialize . . . Go

- out to eat or for coffee
- for a drive
- on a road trip
- to a straight party or dance
- visit relatives or friends
- to the park for a barbecue or picnic
- shopping
- people watching

Toni:

"The most fun thing I can think of is to go to the local pancake house for coffee. Now it's not that I lack imagination or anything. It really is a good time. You get the right bunch of people there and you can literally talk all night! I couldn't believe it would be fun when I first went straight, but we really cover all topics. Nothing is taboo, not even sex or religion."

In the Evening . . . Go

- to a movie
- to a concert
- to a play
- to a dry bar
- formal — dress up and go out
- to a sporting event

Think about it. When was the last time you went to a play? How about a rock, jazz, folk, or classical music concert? If you're interested, the variety of sporting events you can go to are almost endless. Call a local college to see what sports are happening when. It usually doesn't cost much to watch small college sports.

Making a Day of It . . . Go

- to the zoo
- sight-seeing
- to an amusement park
- to county and state fairs
- to local carnivals and festivals
- to dog or horse races
- to the beach, mountains, or country
- camping

So you were going to sit around doing homework all weekend, huh? If you have a little extra cash, a travel agent can tell you about one- or two-day tours in your area.

Something a Little Different . . . Go

- to a museum
- to an art gallery
- to a historical site

If there's a local historical interpretive center in your community — most communities have one — you can learn about what it was like to live in your area one hundred, even two hundred years ago. It's weird to see how much things have changed.

The Great Outdoors

What sport have you always wanted to play? Which one have you wanted to get better at? Well, do it! I'm not saying that you should rush out and join a team at school. Maybe you'd have fun just getting a group together for volleyball.

You don't need a group for all sports either. How about taking tennis lessons or starting a weight lifting regimen?

Not all outdoor activities need to be athletic. How about building a snowman or helping out with some yard work? (Not quite that bored, huh?)

In the Summer . . .
Go

- swimming
- water skiing
- tubing
- sail boating
- surfing
- biking
- running
- horseback riding
- play at a park on the swings and slides
- skateboarding
- fishing
- walking in the woods
- backpacking
- mountain climbing
- hang gliding
- sky diving
- motorcycling

How About Sports? . . .
Play

- volleyball
- tennis
- football
- baseball
- softball
- basketball
- soccer
- golf
- kickball
- broomball
- croquet
- polo
- hackey sack
- horseshoes
- paddle ball
- frisbee

In the Winter . . .
Go

- snowshoeing
- sledding
- build a snowman
- ice fishing
- snowmobiling
- ice skating
- hunting
- skiing, downhill or cross-country

Mark:

"I have never been athletic. I mean, I look athletic because I'm tall and everything, but I don't know the first thing about sports. When I was using, I had no interest in sports, unless you consider throwing a frisbee a sport. Well anyway, just the

209

thought of trying anything athletic shakes me up, you know, I don't want to look stupid. After thinking about it, I just decided that if I'm ever going to learn, I might as well do it now. So this year, I'm trying out for the basketball team. What the hell, if I don't like it, I'll try something else."

The Great Indoors

We are living in a wonderful age. We have so many options for entertainment that people who lived before us didn't have. It's great to turn out all the lights, pop some popcorn, and click on the VCR. Have a different theme each time you get a group together for videos. One week, have all horror flicks. The next week, comedies.

Here are a few more indoor ideas:

In Your Home (or Someone Else's) . . .

- create an eight course meal
- bake cookies
- watch TV
- rent some movies to play on the VCR
- have a food fight
- play cards — poker, kings on the corner, cribbage, Uno, crazy eight, canasta, 500, gin rummy, Old Maid, concentration, go fish, buck yukor
- play board games — Monopoly, Life, Clue, Scrabble, chess, checkers, Scruples, Trivial Pursuit, Pictionary
- play video games

Out and About . . . Go

- shoot pool
- to a gym
- to an arcade
- roller skating
- bowling
- to an aerobics class

Community Involvement

There are a lot of ways to get involved in your community. The best thing to do is call your local United Way and ask them for a list of places that need volunteers. Call your Chamber of Commerce to see if they have a listing too.

Volunteering isn't the only way to get involved, but it's a good place to start.

Think of causes that are important to you and that you wanted to get involved with, but didn't know how. Perhaps you have always wanted to help

- prevent suicide
- prevent teen pregnancies
- homeless people
- victims of battering or sexual assault
- feed the hungry
- preserve the environment
- prevent cruelty to animals

Or work with

- battered women
- Big Brothers or Big Sisters
- accident victims
- AIDS victims
- the blind or physically disabled
- the mentally challenged
- the terminally ill
- the Humane Society
- the Red Cross
- the Salvation Army
- elderly people

This is just a small sampling of ideas. You decide what you would like to be a part of and then pursue it.

LeAnn:

"I never thought I'd be the type to do volunteer work. You know, I figured it meant I'd have to do

something I wouldn't want to do, but it's not like that at all.

"I go to the Humane Society twice a month and help out by walking the cats and dogs, changing their food and water and stuff like that. I love it. My folks won't let me have a cat because my dad's allergic to them, so this is the next best thing."

Self-Improvement

"Self-Improvement" — it seems like these words are on every book and magazine cover.

You may know how to take your inventory and work on character defects, but this is a little different. Ask yourself, *What have I always wished I could do that I'm not able to do now?* Do you want to learn to play guitar, speak French, read tarot cards, or meditate? Do it!

Jason:

"I know this sounds totally weird, but since I went straight, I've learned how to do yoga.

"I sometimes get embarrassed to tell people about it, because they look at me really strange, like I'm some kind of dropout from the sixties or something, but I don't care. I think it's really helped me.

"It's really relaxing and it has taught me a lot about self-discipline. Now I feel like I can learn anything."

Anita:

"I never have been a very good reader. My vocabulary is not that big and sometimes it's frustrating trying to read when I have to look up every other word or read it over and over. That's what I'm working on right now. I'm trying to read more to get better. I might take a class to help me."

Here are some other self-improvement ideas:

1. *Organize your room, your life, or plan for your future.* Maybe you've never thought about going to college or a vocational school. You may want to consider it now. Maybe you don't like school right now, but college is different from high school — there aren't as many rules. You may want to explore different careers and think about which ones you'd like to pursue. Write to different schools to get their literature. Find books at the library that can help you evaluate your interests and decide on a profession.

2. *Read and go to the library.* What do you like to read? Nonfiction, fiction, romance, mysteries, how-to, fantasy, science fiction, self-improvement, humor? Have your librarian help you out. Tell him or her a topic you're interested in and he or she will probably be able to find a long list of books for you to choose from. Learn to use the card catalog or computer at the library so you can find your own books.

3. *Learn to meditate, do yoga, start getting in shape, have a facial, or dye your hair.* Get some meditation tapes and learn to meditate. If done daily, you'll really benefit. It's really a peaceful high. Now may be the time for you to start an exercise program. Treat yourself to a long hot bath and a facial. It's important to treat your body well.

213

4. *Learn to play guitar, drums, harmonica, keyboards, or any other instrument. Then jam.* I think everyone at one time or another has wanted to play some instrument. If you play one already, take the time to improve. Music is a great thing to have in your life.

5. *Learn a new skill or craft.* Photography, macrame, sewing, knitting, needlepoint, dancing, cooking, woodworking, speaking a second language — all these things can help you feel good about yourself as you learn to do them well. If you want to do it, do it! There is no need to be afraid.

By Yourself

Okay, everyone's busy, you're stuck at home with nothing to do. Time to start counting the tiles on the bathroom floor, right? Wrong.

1. *Create something.* Write in a journal, write a resumé, start a photo album or scrapbook, or write some letters. A journal or photo album can reflect your thoughts, attitudes, and emotions. Use your imagination. It can be a record of your life for you to enjoy years from now. Now's the time to start.

2. *Practice the skills you've learned.* If you're just learning to do something — woodworking, macrame, crocheting, gardening, taking pictures — take time to practice and learn to do it well.

3. *Relax.* Soak in the bathtub, meditate, read, sleep, listen to music, or gaze at the stars.

4. *A few more ideas.* Start a collection of something, do crossword puzzles, go to the park, feed the pigeons, or sing.

Relax . . . gaze at the stars

Now It's Your Turn

Hopefully, the ideas listed in this section will get you started. Feel free to add your own ideas to the lists.

As I mentioned earlier in this chapter, whether or not you're bored depends on you. How you spend your time is your choice, but boredom is not an excuse to use.

Keep in mind, too, that it's okay to be bored sometimes.

Sara:

"When I was using, I always had some kind of crisis in my life. Mini disasters were happening all around me and I was usually the one causing them.

"Now I'm straight and sometimes bored, but then I stop and think, *I'm bored, but I feel calm inside and I'm happy* and then I realize that it's nice not to have my life in chaos for a change."

Well, that's all. Now it's up to you. Make your life whatever you want it to be. You *will* get out of life what you put into it.

Conclusion

You may get tired of hearing about having a plan of action, but if you've thought out ahead of time what you need to make being straight easier, then being straight will be easier. So here's the plan for how to stay sober in four easy lessons.

1. *Go to AA or NA*

Okay, so you've heard it a thousand times, but that's because it works. By going to meetings, you're gaining real freedom by stacking the odds for staying off drugs in your favor. AA or NA is a place to have fun, grow, meet people, gain support, and learn. Give it a few weeks at least to start feeling like you belong. If you can, shop around until you find a group you're most comfortable with, then get involved. When you get involved, you help yourself and somebody else. That's how the program works!

2. *Get a Sponsor*

It's nice to have someone you can count on when you have the need. Somebody with more time than you in the program can keep you honest and be objective when you really need support with no strings attached.

3. *Go to Aftercare*

If you have the chance to go to aftercare, go! It's the best way to continue to confront the issues that block your path of living clean and sober. Some problems don't even surface until you've been straight awhile, and you may need professional help to work through them. Aftercare can give you a head start on tackling these problems.

4. *Everyday*

- Make a twenty-four hour commitment to stay straight.
- Put aside some quiet time for meditation or prayer.
- Take an ongoing personal inventory and admit when you're wrong.

- Read program materials, spiritual, or inspirational writings that you find uplifting.
- Make contact with someone who is straight.

The Support of Others

Our greatest inspiration comes from the support of other recovering people. Here are answers that some young people out of treatment for a while gave to the question, "How's it different now that you're sober?"

Heather:

"I just really like myself now."

Tammy:

"I feel more comfortable about my body. I'm going to school. I'm living now instead of surviving."

Justin:

"About two weeks ago, my cousins and I were fishing on this river and my twelve-year-old cousin fell in and got caught in the current. She was moving fast in the water and at first I thought she was kidding around. I didn't realize she was drowning. When it finally hit me, I jumped in and got her and pulled her to shore.

"The whole situation really got to me. I couldn't stop thinking that if I had been using, I would've thought she was goofing off and just laughed. Even if I had realized she was drowning, I probably wouldn't have been able to do anything."

Renee:

"Since I went straight, I've learned so much about myself and how to deal with my feelings.

"I like to dance. I really take it seriously, I mean, I put a lot of time into it. I work out at a studio. I know if I was still using, I wouldn't be dancing."

Nancy:

"The whole life that Brian and I have together is because we are straight. What would be different if I was still using? Well, I wouldn't have a job, a life, a husband. I wouldn't be pregnant . . . well okay, maybe I'd be pregnant, but it probably wouldn't have been planned that way."

Vicki:

"I've got my self-respect now, you know, I don't do things that are embarrassing like I used to when I was wasted."

Tammy:

"I'm feeling real content and peaceful. I was reading the other day and I looked out the window at the sunset. It was so beautiful. Spiritual awakening? Yes! It was a miracle. Such beauty can never be equaled. I felt so high and it was all natural. It was something I never saw while I was on drugs."

What We Tell Ourselves
Is What We Become

A big part of feeling good about being straight is getting in the habit of replacing our addictive thinking with self-affirming thoughts.

Here are a few quotes, sayings, and affirmations that have been useful for me when I needed to remember what clean and sober thinking is.

The Promises

These are promises made in the Big Book to anyone who has been "painstaking about this phase [working Steps One through Nine] of our development."

We are going to know a new freedom and a new happiness. We will not regret the past nor wish to shut the door on it. We will comprehend the word serenity and we will know peace. No matter how far down the scale we have gone, we will see how our experience can benefit others. That feeling of uselessness and self-pity will disappear. We will lose interest in selfish things and gain interest in our fellows. Self-seeking will slip away. Our whole attitude and outlook upon life will change. Fear of people and of economic insecurity will leave us. We will intuitively know how to handle situations which used to baffle us. We will suddenly realize that God is doing for us what we could not do for ourselves.

Are these extravagant promises? We think not. They are being fulfilled among us — sometimes quickly, sometimes slowly. They will always materialize if we work for them.

— Alcoholics Anonymous, 3rd ed., pp. 83-84.

❈   ❈   ❈   ❈   ❈

Look to this day,
For it is life,
The very life of life.
In its brief course lie all
The realities and verities of existence,
The bliss of growth,
The splendor of action,
The glory of power —

For yesterday is but a dream,
And tomorrow is only a vision,
But today, well lived,
Makes every yesterday a dream
of happiness
And every tomorrow a vision of hope.

Look well, therefore, to this day.

— Sanskrit Proverb quoted in
Twenty-Four Hours a Day,
Published by Hazelden
Educational Materials

❋ ❋ ❋ ❋ ❋

I'm Special . . .

In all the world there's nobody like me.
Nobody has my smile.
Nobody has my eyes, nose, hair, or
voice.

I'm Special . . .

No one laughs like me or cries like me.
No one sees things just as I do.
No one reacts just as I would react.

I'm Special . . .

I'm the only one in all creation who has
my set of abilities.
My unique combination of gifts, talents,
and abilities are an original symphony.

I'm Special . . .

I'm rare.
And in all rarity there is great value.
I need not imitate others. I will accept —
yes, celebrate — my differences.

I'm Special . . .

And I'm beginning to see that God made
me special for a very special purpose.
God has a job for me that no one else can
do as well as I do.
Out of all the applicants, only one is
qualified.
That one is me.
Because . . .

I'm Special!

❋　❋　❋　❋　❋

To Be Placed On Your Refrigerator and Read Daily

1. I am a unique and precious human being, always doing the best I can, always growing in wisdom and love.

2. I am in charge of my life.

3. My first responsibility is my own growth and well-being. The better I am to me, the better I will be to others.

4. I refuse to be put down by the attitudes or opinions of others.

5. My actions may be good or bad, but that doesn't make me good or bad.

6. I make my own decisions and assume the responsibility for my mistakes. I need not feel shame about them.

7. I am not free as to the things that will happen to me, but I am 100 percent free as to the attitude I have towards these things. Whether I feel a sense of well-being or suffer depends on my attitude.

8. I do not have to prove myself to anyone. I need only express myself as honestly and effectively as I am capable.

9. I can be free of resentment.

10. My emotional well-being is dependent primarily on how much I love me.

11. I am kind and gentle toward me.

12. I live One Day at a Time and do First Things First.

13. I am patient and serene, for I have the rest of my life in which to grow.

14. Every experience I have in life, even the unpleasant ones, contributes to my learning and growth.

15. No one in the world is more important than I am.

16. My mistakes and failures do not make me a louse, a crumb, or whatever. They only prove that I am imperfect, that is, human. And there is nothing wrong with being human.

17. Once I have reconciled to God and my neighbor, I can be completely free of remorse.

Choosing to Make Our Life Better

Getting sober is a major change in our life, perhaps the most important one we'll make. Any major lifestyle changes can be stressful, but they can also be very rewarding. The alternative to change and growth is to stay the same year after year. With drugs, the alternative can be fatal.

We all make mistakes along the way. That's okay because we're human and not meant to be perfect. But each day we are straight, we can add a new layer of wisdom to our foundation. Our life *will* get better and better.

If I had to pick one message that I hope you got out of this book, that message would be: *you have choices.* Where your life goes from here is up to you. You have incredible potential! I hope you strive for the best.

Have a wonderful sober day — today.

The Twelve Steps Of Alcoholics Anonymous*

1. We admitted we were powerless over alcohol — that our lives had become unmanageable.
2. Came to believe that a Power greater than ourselves could restore us to sanity.
3. Made a decision to turn our will and our lives over to the care of God *as we understood Him.*
4. Made a searching and fearless moral inventory of ourselves.
5. Admitted to God, to ourselves, and to another human being the exact nature of our wrongs.
6. Were entirely ready to have God remove all these defects of character.
7. Humbly asked Him to remove our shortcomings.
8. Made a list of all persons we had harmed, and became willing to make amends to them all.
9. Made direct amends to such people wherever possible, except when to do so would injure them or others.
10. Continued to take personal inventory and when we were wrong promptly admitted it.
11. Sought through prayer and meditation to improve our conscious contact with God *as we understood Him,* praying only for knowledge of His will for us and the power to carry that out.
12. Having had a spiritual awakening as the result of these steps, we tried to carry this message to alcoholics, and to practice these principles in all our affairs.

* The Twelve Steps of A.A. are taken from *Alcoholics Anonymous,* 3rd ed., published by A.A. World Services, Inc., New York, N.Y., 59-60. Reprinted with permission of A.A. World Services, Inc.

The Twelve Traditions Of Alcoholics Anonymous*

1. Our common welfare should come first; personal recovery depends upon A.A. unity.

2. For our group purpose there is but one ultimate authority — a loving God as He may express Himself in our group conscience. Our leaders are but trusted servants; they do not govern.

3. The only requirement for A.A. membership is a desire to stop drinking.

4. Each group should be autonomous except in matters affecting other groups or A.A. as a whole.

5. Each group has but one primary purpose — to carry its message to the alcoholic who still suffers.

6. An A.A. group ought never endorse, finance or lend the A.A. name to any related facility or outside enterprise, lest problems of money, property and prestige divert us from our primary purpose.

7. Every A.A. group ought to be fully self-supporting, declining outside contributions.

8. Alcoholics Anonymous should remain forever non-professional, but our service centers may employ special workers.

9. A.A., as such, ought never to be organized; but we may create service boards or committees directly responsible to those they serve.

10. Alcoholics Anonymous has no opinion on outside issues; hence the A.A. name ought never be drawn into public controversy.

11. Our public relations policy is based on attraction rather than promotion; we need always maintain personal anonymity at the level of press, radio, and films.

12. Anonymity is the spiritual foundation of all our traditions, ever reminding us to place principles before personalities.

---

* The Twelve Traditions of A.A. are taken from *Alcoholics Anonymous*, 3rd ed., published by A.A. World Services, Inc., New York, N.Y., 564. Reprinted with permission.

Index

227

Other titles that will interest you...

Step Meetings for Young People
written by Earl Hipp
photo illustrations by Michael Yencho
Using compelling personal stories, these three pamphlets explain the first three Steps and tackle topics such as unmanageability, powerlessness, honesty, humility, and spirituality.
Order No. 5248   The First Step–HUMILITY
Order No. 5228   The Second Step–HOPE
Order No. 5249   The Third Step–POWER
Order No. 5924   Collection of three pamphlets

Keep It Simple
For every young person concentrating on the fundamentals of recovery, these clearly written meditations encourage understanding of key Twelve Step concepts. Each day's thought includes a suggested activity designed to put recovery principles to work. 400 pp.
Order No. 5066

A Sober Self-Image for Young Adults
by Pamela S.
This pamphlet outlines a self-appraisal process that helps young adults learn the rewards of a sober self-image. 24 pp.
Order No. 1462

For price and order information, please call one of our Telephone Representatives. Ask for a free catalog describing more than 1,500 items available through Hazelden Educational Materials.

HAZELDEN EDUCATIONAL MATERIALS

1-800-328-9000   1-800-257-0070   1-612-257-4010   1-612-257-2195
(Toll Free. U.S. Only)   (Toll Free. MN Only)   (AK and Outside U.S.)   (FAX)

Pleasant Valley Road • P.O. Box 176 • Center City, MN 55012-0176